Daily

GRADE
5

Word Problems
Math

The following illustrations were created by the artists listed (provided through Shutterstock.com) and are protected by copyright: Julianka, Klara Viskova, lilac (page 7); Aluna1 (pages 17–19, 26–28); Pushkin (pages 32–34); vectorpouch (page 40); CNuisin (page 46); bazzier (pages 47–49); ArtHeart (pages 59–61); petovarga (pages 62–64); Lorelyn Medina (pages 65–67); James Daniels (pages 77–79); Moriz (pages 83–85); Anna.zabella (pages 86–88); GraphicsRF (pages 110–112)

Writing: Vicky Shiotsu
Content Editing: Kathleen Jorgensen
Copy Editing: Cathy Harber
Art Direction: Yuki Meyer
Cover Design: Yuki Meyer
Illustration: Bryan Langdo
Design/Production: Jessica Onken
Paula Acojido

EMC 3095

Visit
teaching-standards.com
to view a correlation
of this book.

**Correlated to
Current Standards**

**Congratulations on your purchase of some of the
finest teaching materials in the world.**

*Photocopying the pages in this book
is permitted for <u>single-classroom use only</u>.
Making photocopies for additional classes
or schools is prohibited.*

CPSIA: Sheridan Saline, Inc., Saline, MI, USA [6/2024]

CONTENTS

Introduction

The Value of Using *Daily Word Problems* 4

What's in *Daily Word Problems* 5

How to Use This Book 6

How to Solve Word Problems 7

Scope and Sequence 8

My Progress Chart 10

Week

Week 1 11

Week 2 14

Week 3 17

Week 4 20

Week 5 23

Week 6 26

Week 7 29

Week 8 32

Week 9 35

Week 10 38

Week 11 41

Week 12 44

Week 13 47

Week 14 50

Week 15 53

Week 16 56

Week 17 59

Week 18 62

Week 19 65

Week 20 68

Week 21 71

Week 22 74

Week 23 77

Week 24 80

Week 25 83

Week 26 86

Week 27 89

Week 28 92

Week 29 95

Week 30 98

Week 31 101

Week 32 104

Week 33 107

Week 34 110

Week 35 113

Week 36 116

Answer Key 119

Day-by-Day Skills List 123

The Value of Using *Daily Word Problems*

These 10- to 15-minute daily warm-up activities give students an easy way to use math skills to solve real-world problems.

Daily Word Problems is organized to provide the following:

- a progression from basic to more challenging problems and skills
- practice of grade-level skills and review of previously learned skills
- short, easy-to-read word problems that students can complete independently
- understanding of math concepts, number relationships, and operations
- engaging child-friendly weekly themes

The activities promote the following:

- practice with multiple-step problems
- application of math concepts and operations
- opportunities to explain thinking
- a rigorous student contribution

Getting the most out of *Daily Word Problems*

Try these strategies for extending the *Daily Word Problems* warm-up and incorporating it into your regular math lesson:

- Encourage students to diagram or model the situation in the problem. Provide students with scratch paper if needed.
- Encourage students to ask themselves if their answer makes sense and to check their answer using a different method.
- Invite students to identify patterns, explain concepts, or compare strategies with a partner or in small groups.
- Include discussions as a regular part of your math lessons. Encourage discussion of the situation in the problem, mathematical reasoning, and multiple strategies and approaches to solving the problem.

What's in *Daily Word Problems*

36 Theme-Based Weekly Units

Days 1 through 4

Half-page word problems offer practice using a variety of grade-level or review skills. Work space is included.

Day 5

A full-page activity provides more rigor and often features a chart, graph, map, or other graphic display, a multiple-step problem, or several problems for students to complete.

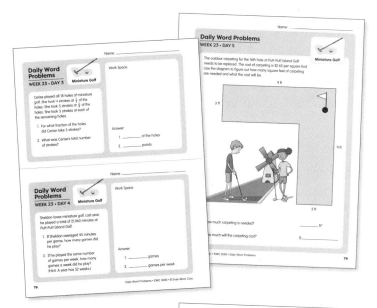

Additional Features

Scope and Sequence

The chart on pages 8 and 9 shows the skills practiced each week.

My Progress Chart

Students can monitor their own progress by recording and analyzing their weekly scores. The blackline master for the chart is on page 10.

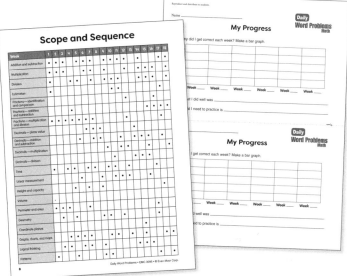

Answer Key

The answer key provides the answer for each day's problem. If a problem is open-ended, a description of the type of valid answer is given. Accept any reasonable response. The answer key begins on page 119.

Day-by-Day Skills List

This list indicates the skills involved in each separate daily problem. It can help you pinpoint and analyze students' strengths and weaknesses. It begins on page 123.

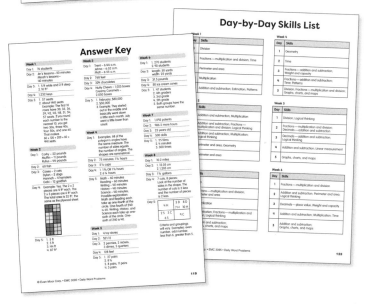

How to Use This Book

1. Reproduce and distribute How to Solve Word Problems on page 7. Use the page to walk your class through the first several problems, using think-alouds to model the Read, Think, and Draw steps.

2. Reproduce and cut apart the problems for each five-day week, or distribute a student book to each student.

3. Preview the page yourself before assigning it to the class. Provide support if there is vocabulary or a concept that students might not be familiar with.

4. Have students work independently, with a partner, or as a class.

   - Remind students that there are usually multiple ways to solve problems. Several of the problems are open-ended and do not have a single correct answer.

   - Students may take some time to figure out how to start; productive struggle is part of the learning process. Guide students with leading questions if needed.

5. Allow time for sharing solutions and problem-solving strategies. Modeling a variety of approaches broadens learning and encourages peer respect and cooperation.

Our Approach

Math exists to solve real-world problems. We encounter many of these problems every day: how much purchases will cost, how long before the school bus arrives, how many eggs are needed for 5 batches of cookies. These problems are not written out for us—they just arise. No one says, "This is going to be an addition problem" or "You'll have to calculate the total needed first and then subtract what you already have." We figure this out from the context and information at hand.

Solving problems, mathematical and otherwise, requires reasoning. The main purpose of word problems is to practice translating the situations in problems into mathematical language. This translation must take place within the context of the problem and show the relationship of the amounts to each other. The problem solver must understand the context and the goal and determine what information is known and what is unknown.

The problems in this book are written as authentically as possible, without intentionally embedding key words as clues to the appropriate operations. Doing so would deprive students of the visualization and analysis practice required to solve real-life problems. Shortcuts for approaching certain types of problems may appear to save time and effort, but they require a lot of memory in the long run, as there are infinite types of problems.

By supporting the higher-order thinking aspects of problem solving, we are teaching students to be thinkers and doers and to believe in their abilities as problem solvers.

Daily Word Problems • EMC 3095 • © Evan-Moor Corporation

How to Solve Word Problems

Word problems are math stories about things that can happen every day in real life. Every problem is different. There is no single way to solve all problems. You need to put yourself in the picture to understand each situation. After you understand what is going on, you can figure out what you need to solve any problem in a math class or in real life.

Read

Read for the basic idea: Read the problem once to see what it's about.

Ask yourself: What's going on in the situation?

Think

Read the problem again more carefully: Put yourself in the situation. Think about the details. Decide what you need to figure out.

Ask yourself: What is the goal of the problem?

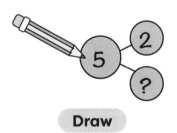

Draw

Draw a picture, diagram, or model of the situation: Each important number should be included, as well as the part you are trying to figure out.

Ask yourself: What do these numbers have to do with each other?

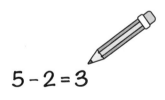

$$5 - 2 = 3$$

Solve

Solve the problem: Decide which operation or operations you need. You can write an equation to help you solve it. **Hint:** Sometimes there will be several steps needed to reach the goal of the problem.

Ask yourself: What do I need to add, subtract, multiply, or divide? Do I need to figure out another number first?

Check

Check your answer: Put your answer in your picture or diagram.

Ask yourself: Does my response answer the question? Does it make sense?

Scope and Sequence

Week	1	2	3	4	5	6	7	8	9	10	11	12	13	14	15	16	17	18
Addition and subtraction	●	●	●		●	●	●		●	●	●	●		●			●	●
Multiplication	●	●	●			●	●		●			●		●	●	●		●
Division	●			●	●		●		●	●	●			●	●			●
Estimation	●									●	●						●	
Fractions—identification and comparison												●				●		
Fractions—addition and subtraction				●											●	●	●	●
Fractions—multiplication and division	●	●	●	●	●	●	●					●					●	
Decimals—place value						●	●	●					●					
Decimals—addition and subtraction					●		●	●			●		●	●	●		●	
Decimals—multiplication									●		●	●			●			●
Decimals—division											●		●	●	●			
Time	●			●	●		●	●		●	●		●			●		
Linear measurement					●			●		●	●	●			●			
Weight and capacity				●			●		●								●	
Volume																		
Perimeter and area	●	●	●				●									●		
Geometry		●		●				●	●		●					●		
Coordinate plane													●					
Graphs, charts, and maps			●	●	●	●			●	●		●		●			●	●
Logical thinking		●	●			●	●		●				●	●	●			
Patterns	●			●					●	●						●		●

Daily Word Problems • EMC 3095 • © Evan-Moor Corporation

19	20	21	22	23	24	25	26	27	28	29	30	31	32	33	34	35	36	Week
●	●			●			●		●			●	●	●				Addition and subtraction
	●	●		●			●	●		●	●	●	●	●	●			Multiplication
●	●	●		●	●	●	●	●			●	●	●		●	●		Division
							●									●		Estimation
											●					●		Fractions—identification and comparison
		●	●	●	●					●		●	●					Fractions—addition and subtraction
●		●	●	●		●	●	●	●	●		●		●		●	●	Fractions—multiplication and division
					●			●	●					●	●			Decimals—place value
	●			●							●		●					Decimals—addition and subtraction
	●			●		●							●					Decimals—multiplication
					●	●		●								●		Decimals—division
●	●					●				●		●				●		Time
	●			●		●					●					●		Linear measurement
		●			●			●		●			●		●			Weight and capacity
					●				●						●		●	Volume
		●	●					●		●				●	●	●		Perimeter and area
		●													●			Geometry
		●				●				●	●					●	●	Coordinate plane
●	●	●	●				●	●		●		●				●		Graphs, charts, and maps
						●			●		●			●			●	Logical thinking
	●		●	●					●			●	●		●		●	Patterns

Name _____

My Progress

How many did I get correct each week? Make a bar graph.

5					
4					
3					
2					
1					

Week ____   Week ____   Week ____   Week ____   Week ____   Week ____

1. A skill that I did well was _____.

2. A skill that I need to practice is _____.

Name _____

Daily Word Problems Math

My Progress

How many did I get correct each week? Make a bar graph.

5					
4					
3					
2					
1					

Week ____   Week ____   Week ____   Week ____   Week ____   Week ____

1. A skill that I did well was _____.

2. A skill that I need to practice is _____.

Name: _____

Daily Word Problems

WEEK 1 • DAY 1

High Notes Music School

High Notes Music School has 210 students who love playing music.

The school offers 15 different classes. Each student takes only one class. If every class has the same number of students, how many students are in each class?

Work Space:

Answer:

_____ students

Name: _____

Daily Word Problems

WEEK 1 • DAY 2

High Notes Music School

Jin takes piano lessons at High Notes Music School. His lessons are 10 minutes longer than Micah's clarinet lessons. Micah's clarinet lessons are $\frac{2}{3}$ the length of Pia's guitar lessons.

If Pia's guitar lessons are 60 minutes long, how long are Jin's and Micah's lessons?

Work Space:

Answer:

Jin's lessons _____

Micah's lessons _____

Name: _____

Daily Word Problems

WEEK 1 • DAY 3

High Notes Music School

Work Space:

The perimeter of a rectangular-shaped electronic keyboard is 14 ft. Its width is 3 ft longer than its depth.

1. How wide and how deep is the keyboard?

2. What is the area of the keyboard?

Answer:

1. _____ ft wide and

   _____ ft deep

2. _____ ft^2

Name: _____

Daily Word Problems

WEEK 1 • DAY 4

High Notes Music School

Work Space:

The piano students at High Notes Music School are having a recital. They will all be playing piano at the same time!

The school has placed 14 pianos on one stage. A piano tuner is coming to tune the pianos. Each piano has 88 keys. How many keys will the tuner tune?

Answer:

_____ keys

 Daily Word Problems • EMC 3095 • © Evan-Moor Corporation

Daily Word Problems

WEEK 1 • DAY 5

High Notes Music School

The High Notes Music School is putting on a concert. The concert will be held at a theater that has 10 rows of seats. There are 30 seats in Row 1. Each row has 3 more seats than the row before it.

1. How many seats are in Row 10?

   _____ seats

2. Estimate how many seats are in the theater.

   _____ seats

   Explain how you got your estimate.

   _____

   _____

   _____

   _____

   _____

   _____

Daily Word Problems

WEEK 2 • DAY 1

Pet Puzzlers

Chloe has three dogs. Corky weighs twice as much as Muffin. Rufus weighs twice as much as Corky.

The total weight of the dogs is 77 pounds. How much does each dog weigh?

Work Space:

Answer:

Corky _____ pounds

Muffin _____ pounds

Rufus _____ pounds

Daily Word Problems

WEEK 2 • DAY 2

Pet Puzzlers

Jake has 30 fish in his aquarium. Emi has $\frac{1}{3}$ the number of fish that Jake has and $\frac{1}{2}$ the number of fish that Tobin has.

If the three students combined all their fish in the school's new aquarium, how many fish would there be?

Work Space:

Answer:

_____ fish

Daily Word Problems

WEEK 2 • DAY 3

Pet Puzzlers

Name: _____

Casey has cats, and Dylan has dogs. They both have the same number of pets. Hannah has hamsters. The number of hamsters equals the total number of cats and dogs. Gabi has goldfish. The number of goldfish is 3 times the number of hamsters.

If there are 20 pets in all, how many pets does each person have?

Work Space:

Answer:

Casey _____ cats

Dylan _____ dogs

Hannah _____ hamsters

Gabi _____ goldfish

Daily Word Problems

WEEK 2 • DAY 4

Pet Puzzlers

Name: _____

Joy is building a doghouse. She needs four rectangular pieces of plywood that each measure 2 ft × 3 ft. She also needs two square pieces that are 2 ft × 2 ft.

The plywood comes in sheets that measure 4 ft × 8 ft. Can Joy use 1 sheet of plywood for all six pieces? Explain your answer.

Work Space:

Use the grid to help you solve the problem.

Answer:

_____

_____

_____

_____

Name: _____

Daily Word Problems
WEEK 2 • DAY 5

Pet Puzzlers

The following shape is a floor plan for a dog run in Jordan's backyard.

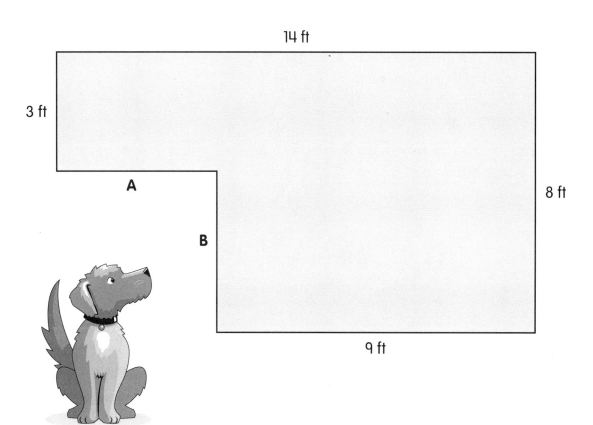

1. What Is the length of **A**? _____ ft

2. What is the length of **B**? _____ ft

3. What is the perimeter of the dog run? _____ ft

4. What is the area of the dog run? _____ ft²

Name: _____

Daily Word Problems

WEEK 3 • DAY 1

Making Chocolate

The Lotta Chocolate Factory opens its doors each day at 7:00 a.m. sharp. Trent, Jehna, and Matt work at the factory. Trent always arrives 16 minutes before the factory opens. Jehna gets there 8 minutes after Trent and 3 minutes before Matt.

At what time do Trent, Jehna, and Matt arrive at the factory?

Work Space:

Answer:

Trent _____ a.m.

Jehna _____ a.m.

Matt _____ a.m.

Name: _____

Daily Word Problems

WEEK 3 • DAY 2

Making Chocolate

The Lotta Chocolate Factory is located in a rectangular building. The distance across the front of the building is 288 feet. The distance from front to back is $\frac{1}{3}$ of that.

Mr. Sweets, the owner of the factory, is going to have a colorful border painted all around the outside of the building. How long will the border be?

Work Space:

Answer:

_____ feet

Daily Word Problems

WEEK 3 • DAY 3

Making Chocolate

The Lotta Chocolate Factory makes Chewy Cherry Chocolates. The chocolates are shipped out in cases. Each case contains 9 boxes. Each box contains 36 chocolates.

How many chocolates are in each case?

Work Space:

Answer:

_____ chocolates

Daily Word Problems

Making Chocolate

WEEK 3 • DAY 4

The Lotta Chocolate Factory sells Gooey Mints, Nutty Chews, and Creamy Caramels. The company sells 4 times as many Gooey Mints as Nutty Chews. It sells half as many Nutty Chews as Creamy Caramels.

If 4,100 boxes of Gooey Mints are sold each month, how many boxes of the other chocolates are sold?

Work Space:

Answer:

Nutty Chews _____ boxes

Creamy Caramels _____ boxes

   Daily Word Problems • EMC 3095 • © Evan-Moor Corporation

Daily Word Problems

WEEK 3 • DAY 5

Making Chocolate

The graph shows last year's chocolate sales for the Lotta Chocolate Factory.

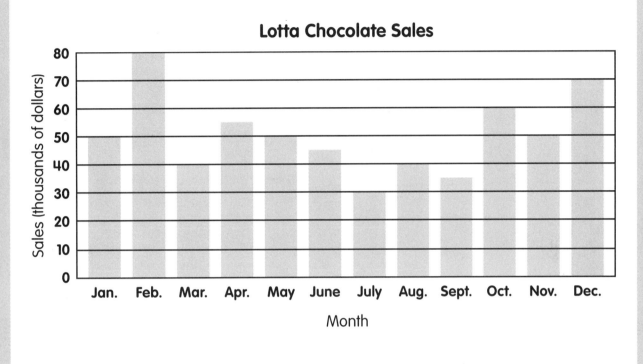

Lotta Chocolate Sales

1. Which month had the greatest number of sales? _____

   How much money was made that month? $_____

2. What was the difference in sales between the month
   with the greatest number and the month with the least? $_____

3. Describe what the sales were like during the middle six months of the year.

   _____

   _____

   _____

Name: _____

Daily Word Problems

WEEK 4 • DAY 1

Homework Time

Sammi has some math homework. She needs to list two ways that all regular polygons are similar. One way is that a regular polygon has sides that are all the same length.

What are two more ways that she could list?

Work Space:

Answer:

_____

_____

_____

_____

Name: _____

Daily Word Problems

WEEK 4 • DAY 2

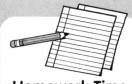

Homework Time

Mr. Judd, Mrs. Kim, and Ms. Sala teach different subjects to the same class. Each teacher gives the same amount of homework every day. Mr. Judd gives twice as much homework as Mrs. Kim. Mrs. Kim gives 5 minutes more than Ms. Sala. Ms. Sala gives 15 minutes of homework each day.

How many minutes of homework do the students get every day? How many hours is that?

Work Space:

Answer:

_____ minutes

_____ hours

Daily Word Problems

WEEK 4 • DAY 3

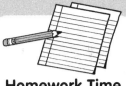

Homework Time

The Trihn triplets were working on their homework together. After a while, Toby, Tyler, and Tim got hungry and decided to share a bag of popcorn.

Each boy ate $1\frac{3}{4}$ cups of popcorn. How many cups of popcorn did the boys eat in all?

Work Space:

Answer:

_____ cups

Daily Word Problems

WEEK 4 • DAY 4

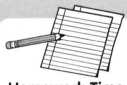

Homework Time

Kalani had a lot of science homework last week. She started off with $\frac{3}{4}$ hour on Monday. Every day after that, she had $\frac{1}{4}$ hour more than the day before.

1. How many hours of science homework did Kalani have on Thursday?

2. How many hours of science homework did she have for the whole school week?

Work Space:

Answer:

1. _____ hours

2. _____ hours

Daily Word Problems

WEEK 4 • DAY 5

Homework Time

The circle graph shows how Bailey spent a total of 240 minutes on homework last week.

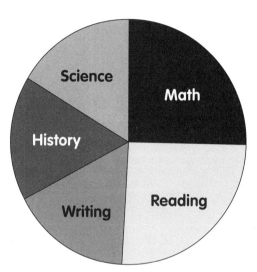

Estimate the number of minutes Bailey spent doing homework in each subject. Then explain how you determined your answers.

Math _____ minutes

Reading _____ minutes

Writing _____ minutes

History _____ minutes

Science _____ minutes

Explanation:

_____

_____

_____

_____

Name: _____

Daily Word Problems

WEEK 5 • DAY 1

Math at the Mall

Max likes mixing math and shopping. Whenever he goes to the mall, he finds ways to do math. One day, Max looked at the store directory and said, "There are 3 times as many clothing stores as shoe stores. There are 4 times as many shoe stores as toy stores."

If there were 48 clothing stores, how many toy stores were there?

Work Space:

Answer:

_____ toy stores

Name: _____

Daily Word Problems

WEEK 5 • DAY 2

Math at the Mall

Max saw that Team Shop was having a huge sale. All sports fan gear was half price.

Max bought three sweatshirts. Their original prices were $15.00, $14.50, and $12.74. How much money did Max save before tax?

Work Space:

Answer:

$_____

Daily Word Problems

WEEK 5 • DAY 3

Math at the **Mall**

While Max was at the mall, he reached into his pocket and pulled out 12 coins. He said, "Wow! I just found $1.67 more to spend!"

Max added, "Hey, the number of pennies equals the number of nickels. The number of nickels added to the number of dimes equals the number of quarters." How many did Max have of each coin?

Work Space:

Answer:

_____ pennies, _____ nickels,

_____ dimes, _____ quarters

Daily Word Problems

WEEK 5 • DAY 4

Math at the **Mall**

Max was walking from one end of the mall to the other end. Just for fun, he took the measurements of five storefronts:

- 23 feet 10 inches
- 25 feet 5 inches
- 20 feet 3 inches
- 28 feet 2 inches
- 30 feet 4 inches

What is the total of all five lengths?

Work Space:

Answer:

_____

Name: _____

Daily Word Problems
WEEK 5 • DAY 5

Math at the Mall

Max's mom works at a women's shoe store at the mall.
One day she kept track of the shoe sizes that were sold.
Then she made a line plot showing the data she collected.

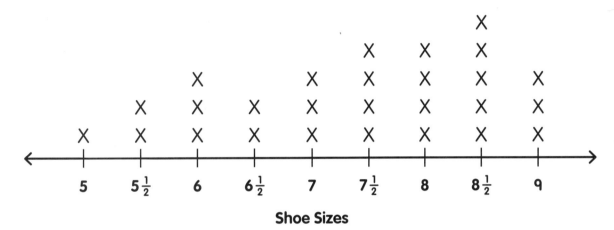

Pairs of Women's Shoes Sold in a Day

1. How many pairs of shoes were sold in all? _____ pairs

2. Which shoe size did most people buy? _____

3. How many pairs of shoes were smaller than size 7? _____ pairs

   How many **more** pairs of shoes were size 7 or larger? _____ pairs

4. If the shoes Max's mom sold had been equally split by size,
   how many of each size would she have sold? _____ pairs

© Evan-Moor Corporation • EMC 3095 • *Daily Word Problems*   **25**

Name: _____

Daily Word Problems

School Picnic

WEEK 6 • DAY 1

Happy Days Elementary School held its annual picnic today, and $\frac{3}{4}$ of the 360 students came. Of the students who came, $\frac{1}{3}$ brought picnic baskets.

1. How many students came?

2. How many students brought picnic baskets?

Work Space:

Answer:

1. _____ students

2. _____ students

Name: _____

Daily Word Problems

School Picnic

WEEK 6 • DAY 2

The picnic area is in the shape of a rectangle. The perimeter of the area is 150 yards. If the length is twice as long as the width, what are the dimensions of the picnic area?

Work Space:

Answer:

length: _____ yards

width: _____ yards

Daily Word Problems • EMC 3095 • © Evan-Moor Corporation

Daily Word Problems

WEEK 6 • DAY 3

School Picnic

Ten friends brought food to the picnic in identical picnic baskets. It turned out that all the picnic baskets had the same weight!

One packed picnic basket weighed 3.15 pounds. What was the total weight of all 10 baskets?

Work Space:

Answer:

_____ pounds

Daily Word Problems

WEEK 6 • DAY 4

School Picnic

The principal and vice principal served ice cream cones at the picnic. It took the principal 10 seconds to make 1 cone. It took the vice principal 15 seconds to make a cone. If the principal and vice principal worked together, how many ice cream cones could they make in 5 minutes?

Work Space:

Answer:

_____ ice cream cones

Name: _____

Daily Word Problems
WEEK 6 • DAY 5

School Picnic

The circle graph shows how many students attended the school picnic.

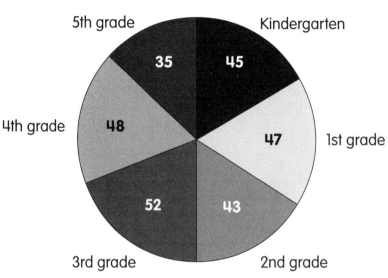

1. How many 1st grade students were at the picnic?   _____ students

2. Were there more 2nd graders or 4th graders?   _____ graders

3. Which grade had the greatest number of students?   _____ grade

4. Which grade had the smallest number of students?   _____ grade

5. Compare the total number of students in Kindergarten through grade 2 with the total number in grades 3 through 5. What do you notice about the two groups?

   _____

   _____

28   Daily Word Problems • EMC 3095 • © Evan-Moor Corporation

Daily Word Problems

WEEK 7 • DAY 1

A Great Inventor

Thomas Edison was one of the world's greatest inventors. He made over a thousand inventions! And he received a patent for many of them. (A patent protects the inventor by preventing others from making the product.) Use the clues to figure out how many U.S. patents he received.

The number of patents is

- 10 times greater than 109.3 and
- 100 times greater than 10.93.

Work Space:

Answer:

_____ patents

Daily Word Problems

WEEK 7 • DAY 2

A Great Inventor

Edison is known for his light bulb. He wasn't the first to make one, but he was the first to create a bulb that worked for more than a few minutes.

Edison made his first light bulb in 1879. It lasted 13.5 hours. The same type of bulb today can last 1,000 hours. How many hours longer is that?

Work Space:

Answer:

_____ more hours

Name: _____

Daily Word Problems

WEEK 7 • DAY 3

A Great Inventor

The first time Edison sold an invention was in 1870. The invention was a stock ticker, which was a device that recorded certain kinds of sales. Edison was paid $40,000 for it. That amount is similar to someone being paid more than $700,000 dollars today!

Edison was born in 1847. How old was he when he sold his stock ticker?

Work Space:

Answer:

_____ years old

Name: _____

Daily Word Problems

WEEK 7 • DAY 4

A Great Inventor

In 1877, Edison invented the phonograph. It was a machine that recorded and played sound. Edison then adapted his invention to make talking dolls. The dolls cost $10 and $20. In today's dollars, that would be over $250 and $500!

It is thought that Edison's company made 10,000 dolls. Only $\frac{1}{20}$ of them were sold. How many dolls was that?

Work Space:

Answer:

_____ dolls

Daily Word Problems

WEEK 7 • DAY 5

A Great Inventor

Edison invented a machine called the kinetoscope. It was a cabinet with a small hole in it. One person at a time could look through the hole and watch a black-and-white film that played for 20 to 30 seconds.

1. It cost a nickel to watch Edison's films. If you had $1.25, how many of his films could you watch? _____ films

2. Suppose 12 people were in line to watch one of Edison's 20-second films. How many minutes would it take for all the people in line to see the movie? _____ minutes

3. Today, a movie ticket can cost as much as $15.00. How many times could a person watch Edison's film for that price? _____ times

Daily Word Problems

WEEK 8 • DAY 1

Alice's Adventures

Alice's Adventures in Wonderland is a tale of a girl who enters a land filled with odd characters.

In the story, Alice follows a talking White Rabbit down a rabbit hole and falls a very long way. Suppose she first fell 1.2 miles, then 3.4 miles, and then 5.6 miles after that before landing. How many miles would she have traveled?

Work Space:

Answer:

_____ miles

Daily Word Problems

WEEK 8 • DAY 2

Alice's Adventures

Alice drinks from a bottle marked DRINK ME and becomes very small. Then she eats a little cake with the note EAT ME and grows very tall!

1. Suppose Alice's actual height was 120.5 cm. If she shrank to $\frac{1}{10}$ of her height, how small did she become?

2. Suppose Alice grew to 10 times her normal size. How tall did she become?

Work Space:

Answer:

1. _____ cm

2. _____ cm

Daily Word Problems

WEEK 8 • DAY 3

Alice's Adventures

Name: _____

Alice meets the March Hare, the Hatter, and the Dormouse at a tea party. Time has stopped at 6:00 there, so it's always teatime.

If the March Hare, the Hatter, and the Dormouse each drink 2 cups of tea every hour, how many gallons would they drink in 4 hours?

2 cups = 1 pint
2 pints = 1 quart
4 quarts = 1 gallon

Work Space:

Answer:

_____ gallons

Daily Word Problems

WEEK 8 • DAY 4

Alice's Adventures

Name: _____

Alice has tea with the March Hare, the Hatter, and the Dormouse. Suppose they offer her cakes that are cut into triangular pieces like this:

How many cuts would a 10-sided cake have? How many triangular pieces would there be? Explain how you know.

Work Space:

Answer:

_____ cuts, _____ pieces

_____

_____

_____

_____

_____

_____

Daily Word Problems

WEEK 8 • DAY 5

Alice's Adventures

Alice meets the Queen of Hearts and sees that her servants are playing cards! She groups them using the features of suit color and number value.

Look at the categories for each row and column. Write each card in the correct box. For example, the 2 of spades is in the lower-left box because spades is a black suit and 2 is a factor of 12.

	factor of 12	not a factor of 12
red suit		
black suit	2 S	

Suits

Black: ♠ Spades   ♣ Clubs

Red: ♥ Hearts   ♦ Diamonds

Now write your own categories for grouping the cards. Then list the cards in the boxes.

Daily Word Problems

WEEK 9 • DAY 1

Amusement Park

Ana's dad is going to take her to a new amusement park. He looked up the park on a map. He saw that the park was in the shape of a quadrilateral. The north and south sides were parallel. The east and west sides were not, though. However, the west side was perpendicular to both the north and the south side.

What name describes the shape? Draw a picture of it.

Work Space:

Answer:

The shape is a _____.

Daily Word Problems

WEEK 9 • DAY 2

Amusement Park

A merry-go-round at the amusement park has 48 horses. Each horse holds 1 child. The ride lasts 4 minutes, and it takes 2 minutes to change all the riders.

If all the horses have a passenger each time, how many children can ride the merry-go-round in half an hour?

Work Space:

Answer:

_____ children

Daily Word Problems

WEEK 9 • DAY 3

Amusement Park

Ana went on the Spin 'n' Grin ride. As her car rode along the track, it spun her 36 times to the left and 28 times to the right. Ana loved the ride so much that she went on it several times!

Altogether, Ana spun 144 times to the left and 112 times to the right. How many times did she go on the ride?

Name: _____

Work Space:

Answer:

_____ times

Daily Word Problems

WEEK 9 • DAY 4

Amusement Park

Ana is meeting two friends at the amusement park. The three of them want to go on 7 rides. Each ride costs 5 tickets. The tickets are sold in packs of 20 for $5 or individually for 40¢ each.

1. How many tickets will they need?

2. What is the least expensive way to buy the tickets without having any tickets left over? How much will the tickets cost?

Name: _____

Work Space:

Answer:

1. _____ tickets

2. _____

_____

_____

_____

Total cost: $_____

Daily Word Problems • EMC 3095 • © Evan-Moor Corporation

Daily Word Problems

WEEK 9 • DAY 5

Amusement Park

A Ferris wheel operator kept track of how many people rode the ride each day. When he looked at the numbers, he saw an interesting pattern.

Day	Monday	Tuesday	Wednesday	Thursday
Number of Riders	210	220	240	270

1. What pattern do you see?

   _____

   _____

2. If the pattern continued, how many riders could be expected to ride the Ferris wheel on Friday? _____ riders

3. On what day would there be twice as many riders as there were on Monday?

   _____

   How many riders would there be?

   _____ riders

Daily Word Problems

WEEK 10 • DAY 1

Roller Coasters

The first roller coaster in America opened at Coney Island in New York in 1884. It cost a nickel per ride. The roller coaster was so popular that the owner made $600 a day!

How many rides had to be sold every day for the owner to make that much money?

Work Space:

Answer:

_____ rides

Daily Word Problems

WEEK 10 • DAY 2

Roller Coasters

In 2000, Japan's Steel Dragon became the longest roller coaster in the world. Its track is 8,133 feet long!

1. One mile equals 5,280 feet. How much longer than a mile is the Steel Dragon?

2. Is your answer to problem 1 less than or greater than half a mile? Explain how you can use estimation to help you.

Work Space:

Answer:

1. _____ feet longer

2. _____

_____

_____

_____

Daily Word Problems

WEEK 10 • DAY 3

Roller Coasters

Work Space:

California's oldest roller coaster is the Giant Dipper. It was built in 1924 in Santa Cruz. When it opened, the ticket price was $0.15.

In 2014, the price of a ticket was $6. How many times greater was the 2014 price than the original ticket price?

Answer:

_____ times greater

Daily Word Problems

WEEK 10 • DAY 4

Roller Coasters

Work Space:

Wooden roller coasters run on a wooden track. Outlaw Run is a wooden roller coaster in Branson, Missouri. Its track is 2,937 feet long. GhostRider is a wooden roller coaster in Buena Park, California. Its track is 4,533 feet long.

Estimate how many feet shorter Outlaw Run is than GhostRider. Explain how you got your estimate.

Answer:

about _____ feet shorter

_____

_____

_____

_____

Daily Word Problems

WEEK 10 • DAY 5

Roller Coasters

Six Flags Magic Mountain in Southern California has more roller coasters than any other amusement park. Some are listed on the chart.

Roller Coaster	Opening Day	Length of Track (feet)	Length of Ride (minutes and seconds)
Gold Rusher	May 29, 1971	2,590	2:30
Goliath	Feb. 11, 2000	4,500	3:00
New Revolution	May 8, 1976	3,457	2:12
Twisted Colossus	May 23, 2015	4,990	3:40
Viper	April 7, 1990	3,830	2:30
X2	Jan. 12, 2002	3,610	2:20

1. The Gold Rusher was the park's first roller coaster. It opened in 1971. How many years later did Goliath open?

   _____ years

2. Which roller coaster on the chart has the longest track?

   _____

   How much longer is the longest track than the shortest track?

   _____ feet longer

3. Suppose you went on each of the roller coasters listed on the chart. What is the total amount of time you would spend on the tracks?

   _____ minutes, _____ seconds

Daily Word Problems • EMC 3095 • © Evan-Moor Corporation

Daily Word Problems

WEEK 11 • DAY 1

At the Library

Work Space:

The Booktown Library has four shelves of books along one wall. On the top shelf, 21 of the 120 books have been checked out. On the two shelves below, 9 of the 140 books and 12 of the 105 books have been checked out. On the bottom shelf, 25 of the 115 books have been checked out.

Estimate how many books remain on the shelves. Round the numbers to help you.

Answer:

about _____ books

Daily Word Problems

WEEK 11 • DAY 2

At the Library

Work Space:

Miss Paige, the librarian, was checking the thicknesses of several books and found that the average thickness was 2.1 cm. She found this by adding the thicknesses of five books and dividing the sum by 5.

Four books had these measures: 1.6 cm, 1.9 cm, 2.2 cm, and 2.5 cm. What was the thickness of the fifth book she measured?

Answer:

_____ cm

Daily Word Problems

WEEK 11 • DAY 3

At the Library

Work Space:

The library is purchasing 130 new children's books this month.

Half the books will cost $4.00 each, and the other half will cost $4.25 each. How much will the library spend to buy the new books?

Answer:

$_____

Daily Word Problems

WEEK 11 • DAY 4

At the Library

Work Space:

A bookcase in the library has five shelves. The bottom shelf is 3 inches off the ground. The second shelf is 1 foot 5 inches above the bottom shelf. The third is 1 foot 4 inches above the second. The fourth is 1 foot 3 inches above the third. The top shelf is 1 foot 2 inches above the fourth.

How high off the ground is the top shelf?

Answer:

_____ feet _____ inches

Daily Word Problems

WEEK 11 • DAY 5

At the Library

The library just received ten new tables. The top of each table is a trapezoid formed by three triangles, as shown at right. The librarian grouped four tables to form a larger trapezoid. Then she put six different tables together to form a parallelogram. Color the triangular grid below to show how the tables may have been grouped.

= 1 table

Daily Word Problems

WEEK 12 • DAY 1

Dog Walking

Work Space:

Pavel started a dog-walking business called Happy Tails. He designed a flier to advertise to his neighbors and had 100 fliers printed.

The copy center charged Pavel 12¢ each for the first 20 fliers and then 8¢ for each additional one after that. What was the total cost of the fliers?

Answer:

$ _____

Daily Word Problems

WEEK 12 • DAY 2

Dog Walking

Work Space:

Pavel starts walking dogs at 3:15 p.m. each day after school. He is done by 6:00 p.m. so he can be home in time for dinner.

Pavel schedules each dog walk for a half hour. He also allows himself 15 minutes between walks to travel to the next customer's home. What is the maximum number of dogs Pavel can walk before dinnertime each day?

Answer:

_____ dogs

Daily Word Problems

WEEK 12 • DAY 3

Dog Walking

Work Space:

Pavel charges $6 to walk a small dog and $10 to walk a large dog. Last week, he walked the same number of small dogs as large dogs. He earned a total of $96.

How many small dogs and large dogs did Pavel walk last week?

Answer:

_____ small dogs

_____ large dogs

Daily Word Problems

WEEK 12 • DAY 4

Dog Walking

Work Space:

When Pavel goes dog-walking, he travels at least $\frac{3}{4}$ mile with each dog.

1. If Pavel walked 3 dogs in one day, how many miles did he cover?

2. If Pavel walked 6 miles in 2 days, how many dogs did he walk?

Answer:

1. _____ miles

2. _____ dogs

Name: ______________________________

Daily Word Problems

WEEK 12 • DAY 5

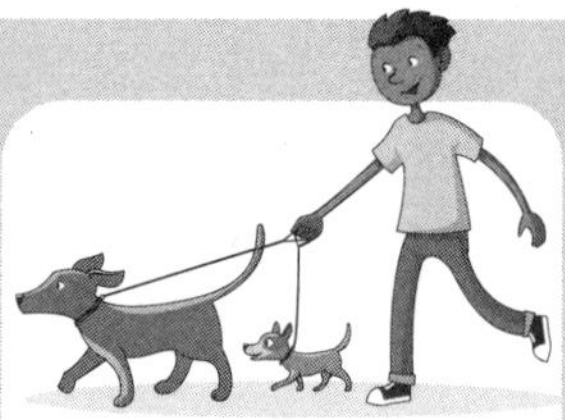

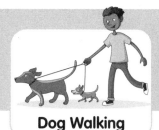

Dog Walking

Pavel's Happy Tails dog-walking business is doing well! The graph shows how many dogs he walks each week.

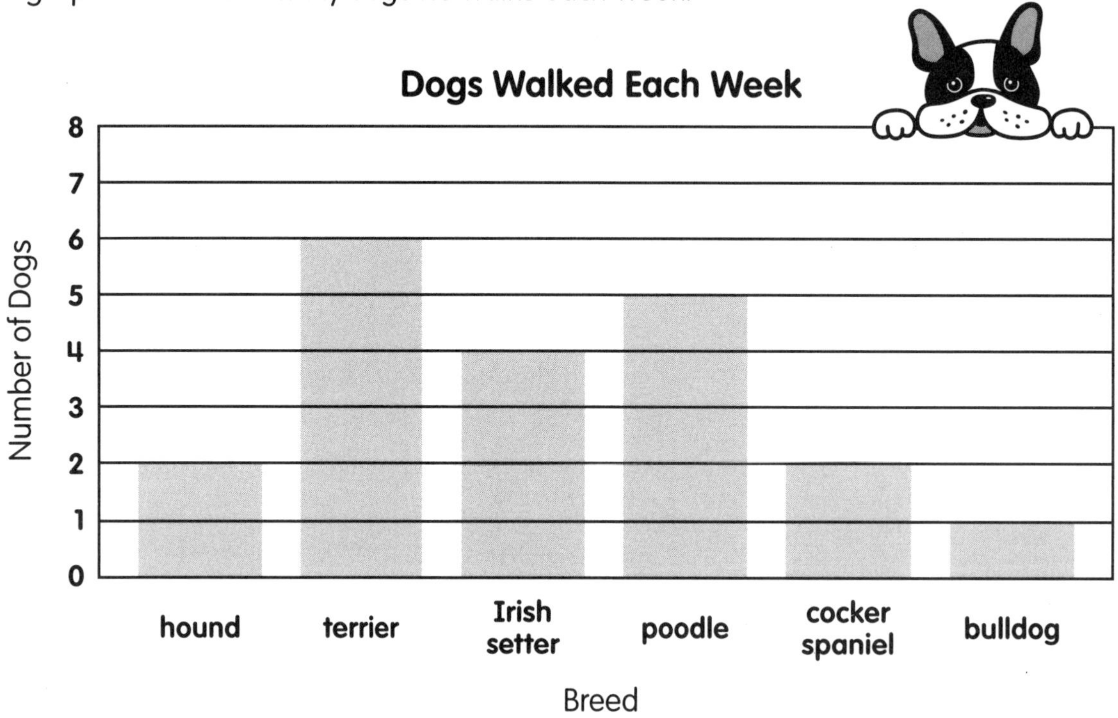

Write the fraction that best compares the numbers described below. The first one has been done for you.

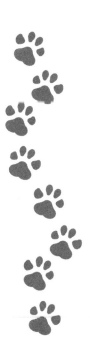

1. The number of hounds is $\frac{1}{2}$ the number of Irish setters.
2. The number of bulldogs is __________ the number of poodles.
3. The number of cocker spaniels is __________ the number of terriers.
4. The number of poodles is __________ the total number of dogs.
5. The number of cocker spaniels is __________ the total number of dogs.

Name: _____

Daily Word Problems

WEEK 13 • DAY 1

Race Car Math

Zip, Dash, and Boomer are racing their cars around a track. Zip and Dash have completed the same number of laps. Boomer has completed 6 more laps than Zip and Dash have each completed. The total number of completed laps is 219 laps.

How many laps has each racer completed?

Work Space:

Answer:

Zip _____ laps

Dash _____ laps

Boomer _____ laps

Name: _____

Daily Word Problems

WEEK 13 • DAY 2

Race Car Math

Ace loves racing cars! She has entered four different races so far this year. Ace drove 275 miles in the first race and 255 miles in the second race. She drove the same number of miles in the third and fourth races.

Ace drove an average of 250 miles per race. How many miles did she drive in the third and fourth races?

Work Space:

Answer:

third race _____ miles

fourth race _____ miles

Name: _____

Daily Word Problems

WEEK 13 • DAY 3

Race Car Math

During a race, drivers make a pit stop to refuel and change the tires on their cars. Manny's crew was able to get his car back into the race 0.6 second faster than Kelly's crew. Kelly's crew took 1.1 seconds longer than Sherman's crew. Sherman's crew took 7.9 seconds to complete the pit stop.

How many seconds did Manny's crew take?

Work Space:

Answer:

_____ seconds

Name: _____

Daily Word Problems

WEEK 13 • DAY 4

Race Car Math

Enrico's car uses 45.5 gallons of fuel per race. Courtney's car uses 48 gallons of fuel per race.

After how many races will Courtney's car have used 25 more gallons of fuel than Enrico's car?

Work Space:

Answer:

_____ races

Daily Word Problems

WEEK 13 • DAY 5

Race Car Math

Read the clues and fill in the chart to determine what position five racers placed in a race. When you know that a name and a position **don't** go together, make an **X** under that position and across from that name. When you know that a name and a position **do** go together, write **YES** in that box.

Clues:

- Dash did not come in 3rd place.
- Ace and Miles did not come in 1st or 5th place.
- Boomer finished the race ahead of Miles but behind Ace.
- Zip did not come in 1st place.

	1st place	2nd place	3rd place	4th place	5th place
Ace					
Boomer					
Dash					
Miles					
Zip					

Write the name of each racer beside the correct place.

1st place _____   4th place _____

2nd place _____   5th place _____

3rd place _____

Daily Word Problems

WEEK 14 • DAY 1

A-OK Arcade

Name: _____

Work Space:

Ian wanted to play some new video games at the A-OK Arcade. He spent $3.75 to buy 15 game tokens.

1. How much did each game token cost?

2. If Ian paid with a five-dollar bill, how many more game tokens could he buy with the change he got back?

Answer:

1. $_____

2. _____ more game tokens

Daily Word Problems

WEEK 14 • DAY 2

A-OK Arcade

Name: _____

Work Space:

Yuka's high score on the Kaboom! video game was 345,500. Justin's high score was 415,200. Amira's high score was exactly halfway between Yuka's and Justin's high scores.

What was Amira's high score?

Answer:

_____

Daily Word Problems • EMC 3095 • © Evan-Moor Corporation

Daily Word Problems

WEEK 14 • DAY 3

A-OK Arcade

Name: _____

The triplets Kevin, Kara, and Kai went to the A-OK Arcade together. Kevin spent $4.25. Kara spent $2.75 more than Kai, who spent $1.55 less than Kevin.

How much money did the triplets spend altogether?

Work Space:

Answer:

$_____

Daily Word Problems

WEEK 14 • DAY 4

A-OK Arcade

Name: _____

Space Race is the most popular game at the A-OK Arcade. The game awards 125 points for each spaceship that a player passes during a race.

When Allie played the game for the first time, she passed 18 spaceships! How many points did she earn?

Work Space:

Answer:

_____ points

Daily Word Problems

WEEK 14 • DAY 5

A-OK Arcade

The shaded box on the map shows the location of the
A-OK Arcade. Each space on the map represents one block,
and each letter represents a different friend's house.

North ↑

				J			
		F					N
					A-OK		
A						M	
	D	E	G				O
				I		L	
	C						
			H		K		
	B						P

Kenichi's mom will drive Kenichi and
his two friends to the arcade. She
followed these directions:

- Leave home. Go 1 block north.
- Go 2 blocks west to pick up Latoya.
- Go 2 blocks north.
- Go 6 blocks east to pick up Jalil.
- Go 3 blocks north.
- Go 2 blocks west to the arcade.

1. What letter on the map represents Kenichi's house? _____

2. What letter on the map represents Latoya's house? _____

3. What letter on the map represents Jalil's house? _____

Name: _____

Daily Word Problems

Loads of Laundry

WEEK 15 • DAY 1

Jessie and her family had been very busy and weren't able to wash their dirty clothes for several weeks. Now that they finally have time, they've discovered they have 544 items of clothing to wash!

Jessie's family figures that a single load can hold about 32 items. How many loads will the family have to do to wash all the laundry?

Work Space:

Answer:

_____ loads

Name: _____

Daily Word Problems

Loads of Laundry

WEEK 15 • DAY 2

Mischa just went away to college this fall and had to buy her own laundry soap and fabric softener. The laundry soap was twice the cost of the fabric softener. The total cost of the two items was $9.45.

What were the prices of the laundry soap and the fabric softener?

Work Space:

Answer:

laundry soap $_____

fabric softener $_____

Daily Word Problems

WEEK 15 • DAY 3

Loads of Laundry

Jamael is waiting for his laundry to dry. In the dryer are 24 socks that are identical except for their color. There are 6 yellow socks, 8 blue socks, and 10 black socks.

Suppose Jamael reaches into the dryer and pulls out one sock at a time without looking. What is the minimum number of socks he will need to pull out to be sure he has a matching pair? How do you know?

Work Space:

Answer:

_____

_____

_____

_____

_____

Daily Word Problems

WEEK 15 • DAY 4

Loads of Laundry

Bubbly Suds Laundromat has 10 washing machines standing in a single row against one wall. There is a $\frac{1}{4}$ inch of space between each machine and the next one.

Each machine is 2 feet 3 inches wide. How long is the entire row of washing machines?

Work Space:

Answer:

_____ feet _____ inches

Name: _____

Daily Word Problems

WEEK 15 • DAY 5

Loads of **Laundry**

Bubbly Suds Laundromat is open 7 days a week from 6:00 a.m. to 9:00 p.m. The laundromat operates a total of 24 large washing machines.

1. Each washing machine washes an average of 18 loads a day. How many loads of laundry are washed daily on average?

    _____ loads

2. Customers pay $1.75 for each load of laundry. How much money do the 24 washing machines bring in every day?

    $_____

3. The owner of Bubbly Suds Laundromat is thinking of raising the price of a load of laundry by 10¢. How much more money would the laundromat make every day?

    $_____ more

Daily Word Problems

WEEK 16 • DAY 1

Space Vacation

Commander Zander flew a spaceship of excited tourists to the planet Zee. The spacecraft traveled at a speed of 40 kilometers a second.

1. How far did the spaceship travel in 1 minute?

2. How far did it travel in 1 hour?

Work Space:

Answer:

1. _____ kilometers

2. _____ kilometers

Daily Word Problems

WEEK 16 • DAY 2

Space Vacation

When Commander Zander's spaceship landed on the planet Zee, 32 guides arrived to take the tourists sightseeing. There were 1,440 tourists aboard the spaceship. The commander divided them into 32 equal groups.

How many tourists were in each group?

Work Space:

Answer:

_____ tourists

Name: _____

Daily Word Problems

WEEK 16 • DAY 3

Space Vacation

Thirty-two groups of tourists split up to explore the planet Zee.

- $\frac{3}{16}$ went to see Liquid Lava Lake.
- $\frac{1}{16}$ went to Yucky Mucky Swamp.
- $\frac{5}{16}$ went to hear the Talking Forest.
- The rest went hiking to Laser Falls.

1. What fraction went to Laser Falls?

2. Did more tourists go to the Talking Forest or to Laser Falls?

Work Space:

Answer:

1. _____

2. _____

Name: _____

Daily Word Problems

WEEK 16 • DAY 4

Space Vacation

Some tourists were exploring the Talking Forest when they saw a herd of 100 Zingalings. They observed that $\frac{3}{5}$ of the herd was yellow with green spots, while the rest were blue with red spots.

Were there more yellow Zingalings than blue ones, or were there more blue Zingalings than yellow ones? Explain how you know.

Work Space:

Answer:

_____

_____

_____

_____

Daily Word Problems

WEEK 16 • DAY 5

Space Vacation

The tourists on planet Zee noticed an unusual flower called the pentagonia. The center of the flower was surrounded by 5 petals that were pentagons. The center was also a pentagon. All 6 shapes on each flower were the same size and shape.

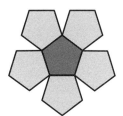

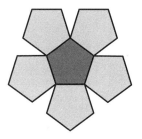

Fill in the table to show how the perimeter of the center and the perimeter of the flower's outline are related. One row has been done for you.

Length of One Side of Pentagon	Perimeter of Center	Perimeter of Flower
1 cm	5 cm	20 cm
2 cm		
3 cm		
4 cm		

1. How is the perimeter of the flower related to the perimeter of its center?

_____

_____

2. The largest pentagonia on the planet Zee has a center whose side measures 25 cm.

What is the perimeter of the flower's center? _____ cm

What is the perimeter of the flower? _____ cm

Name: _____

Daily Word Problems

WEEK 17 • DAY 1

Oh-So-Good Pizza

Leo and four of his friends went to Oh-So-Good Pizza, their favorite pizza place. As usual, they ordered three large pizzas.

If the five friends shared the pizzas equally and there were no slices left over, what fraction of a pizza did each person get?

Work Space:
Draw a picture of the pizzas to help you solve the problem.

Answer:

_____ of a pizza

Name: _____

Daily Word Problems

WEEK 17 • DAY 2

Oh-So-Good Pizza

Tonya and her parents went to Oh-So-Good Pizza for lunch. They ordered a large pizza for $18.99, a pitcher of lemonade for $6.75, and three side salads for $2.50 each.

If the family paid for the meal with two twenty-dollar bills, how much change did they receive?

Work Space:

Answer:

$_____

Name: _____

Daily Word Problems

Oh-So-Good Pizza

WEEK 17 • DAY 3

Pedro makes pizzas at Oh-So-Good Pizza. The chart shows how much cheese he uses on each size.

12-inch pizza	5.25 oz of cheese
14-inch pizza	7.25 oz of cheese
16-inch pizza	10.5 oz of cheese

Pedro grates 16-ounce blocks of cheese. If he makes 2 of each size of pizza, estimate how many blocks of cheese he will need.

Work Space:

Answer:

_____ blocks of cheese

Name: _____

Daily Word Problems

Oh-So-Good Pizza

WEEK 17 • DAY 4

The pizza crust at Oh-So-Good Pizza comes in three thicknesses: $\frac{1}{8}$-inch thick, $\frac{1}{4}$-inch thick, and $\frac{1}{2}$-inch thick.

Suppose you stacked the three pizza crusts one on top of the other.

1. Would your stack be greater than or less than 1 inch tall?

2. How much greater or how much less than 1 inch would it be?

Work Space:

Answer:

1. _____

2. _____

Daily Word Problems

WEEK 17 • DAY 5

Oh-So-Good Pizza

The fifth-grade classes at an elementary school ordered 16 pizzas for a party. Use the clues to determine how many of each kind of pizza they bought.

Clues:

- One fourth of the pizzas have just cheese.
- One third of the remaining pizzas have pepperoni only.
- One fourth of the remaining pizzas have mushrooms and sausage.
- One half of the remaining pizzas have ham and pineapple.
- One third of the remaining pizzas have mushrooms and olives.
- Half of the remaining pizzas have hamburger, while the other half have bacon and onion.

Write how many there are of each kind of pizza.

Type of Pizza	Number of Pizzas
cheese only	_____
pepperoni only	_____
mushroom and sausage	_____
ham and pineapple	_____
mushroom and olive	_____
hamburger	_____
bacon and onion	_____

Name: _____

Daily Word Problems

WEEK 18 • DAY 1

Recycling Projects

The students at Pine View School collected newspapers for a four-week recycling project. During the first week, they collected 114 pounds of newspapers. For each of the next three weeks, they doubled the previous week's amount of newspapers collected.

How many pounds of newspapers did the school collect altogether?

Work Space:

Answer:

_____ pounds

Name: _____

Daily Word Problems

WEEK 18 • DAY 2

Recycling Projects

Pine View School's principal found out that the school would receive 3 cents for every 2 aluminum cans that were collected for recycling.

The school collected 15,600 cans. How much money did it receive?

Work Space:

Answer:

$ _____

Name: _____

Daily Word Problems

WEEK 18 • DAY 3

Recycling Projects

The teachers at Pine View School were recycling their scrap paper by placing it in large bins. They discovered that a full bin weighed 360.2 pounds!

The teachers recycled 15 bins of paper last year. What was the total weight of all the paper?

Work Space:

Answer:

_____ pounds

Name: _____

Daily Word Problems

WEEK 18 • DAY 4

Recycling Projects

The members of the Pine View School art club needed paper towel tubes for a project using recycled materials. They posted a sign asking students for tubes. Each of the school's 574 students brought in 4 tubes!

How many paper towel tubes did the art club collect?

Work Space:

Answer:

_____ tubes

Daily Word Problems

WEEK 18 • DAY 5

Recycling Projects

Pine View School's 3rd- through 5th-grade classes collected empty plastic water bottles for a recycling project last week. The line plot shows the weights of the classes' collections.

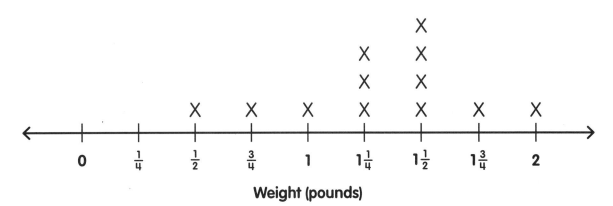

Plastic Bottle Collections

Weight (pounds)

1. How much did the heaviest bottle collection weigh? _____ pounds

2. What was the difference in weight between the heaviest collection and the lightest collection? _____ pounds

3. How many classes collected at least $1\frac{1}{2}$ pounds of bottles? _____ classes

4. What was the total weight of all the bottles? _____ pounds

Daily Word Problems • EMC 3095 • © Evan-Moor Corporation

Daily Word Problems

WEEK 19 • DAY 1

Family Reunion

Work Space:

Batoul and her family were traveling by car to a family reunion. They traveled 540 miles the first day and 480 miles the second day.

If Batoul and her family averaged 60 miles an hour, how many hours were they on the road?

Answer:

_____ hours

Daily Word Problems

WEEK 19 • DAY 2

Family Reunion

Work Space:

Simon and his relatives were gathering for a family reunion. There were 9 pairs of aunts and uncles. For every 3 uncles, there were 4 cousins. There were also 2 grandparents, plus Simon's parents and sister.

How many people were at the reunion?

Answer:

_____ people

Name: _____

Daily Word Problems

WEEK 19 • DAY 3

Family Reunion

Work Space:

Andrei and his family are driving to their family reunion. The drive will take $6\frac{1}{2}$ hours. They plan to take a 10-minute stop for gas halfway through the trip. They also plan to stop 45 minutes for lunch.

Andrei and his family do not want to be late for the huge dinner that is being planned. What is the latest time they can leave home in order to arrive at the reunion by 5:00 p.m.?

Answer:

_____

Name: _____

Daily Word Problems

WEEK 19 • DAY 4

Family Reunion

Work Space:

There are 16 families attending the Robles family reunion. The relatives plan to split the cost of a special gift for the great-grandparents.

The gift costs $520. How much will each family contribute?

Answer:

$ _____

Daily Word Problems • EMC 3095 • © Evan-Moor Corporation

Daily Word Problems

WEEK 19 • DAY 5

Family Reunion

There were 48 people at Alison's family reunion. The circle graph shows information about the ages of the people who attended.

1. How many people were under 10 years old?

   _____ people

2. How many people were over 50 years old?

   _____ people

3. How many more people were between 21 and 50 years old than between 11 and 20 years old?

   _____ more

4. Alison's Aunt Irene and Uncle Roger, who are both 38 years old, and their two children, who are 9 and 12 years old, could not come to the reunion. If they had come, what would the fractions have been in each section of the circle graph?

   under 10 years old: _____   21 to 50 years old: _____

   11 to 20 years old: _____   over 50 years old: _____

Daily Word Problems

WEEK 20 • DAY 1

Bus Travel

The buses in Pleasant Acres are 45 feet long and 9 feet wide. A blue stripe will be painted around the outside of each bus.

1. What will the total length of the stripe on each bus be in feet?

2. What is that length in inches?

Work Space:

Answer:

1. _____ feet

2. _____ inches

Daily Word Problems

WEEK 20 • DAY 2

Bus Travel

Pleasant Acres has a fleet of 47 buses. Each bus can seat 42 people.

Suppose all the buses were in use at the same time and each bus were full. How many people would be riding the buses?

Work Space:

Answer:

_____ people

 Daily Word Problems • EMC 3095 • © Evan-Moor Corporation

Name: _____

Daily Word Problems

Bus Travel

WEEK 20 • DAY 3

Azad's class is going on a field trip. The students will ride the bus twice, once going and once coming back. A one-way bus trip costs $0.50 per student and $1.25 per adult.

There are 23 students, 1 teacher, and 3 parents going. How much money will the bus fare cost?

Work Space:

Answer:

$_____

Name: _____

Daily Word Problems

Bus Travel

WEEK 20 • DAY 4

Gerry is a bus driver. He drives around the city five days a week. Gerry takes his bus to a bus repair shop for service and repairs every 6,000 miles. He has driven his bus 28,970 miles so far.

How many times has Gerry taken his bus to the shop?

Work Space:

Answer:

_____ times

Name: _____

Daily Word Problems

WEEK 20 • DAY 5

Bus Travel

A city bus picks up people at Stop A, the first stop on its route. The bus continues on to Stops B, C, D, and E, where it picks up or drops off passengers. After Stop E, the bus travels back to Stop A and starts all over again. It follows this pattern until 7:00 p.m.

The schedule shows when the bus leaves the different stops.

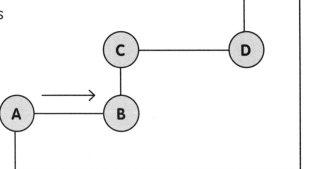

Bus Departures from Stops A, B, C, D, E

A	B	C	D	E
7:00 a.m.	7:05 a.m.	7:10 a.m.	7:15 a.m.	7:20 a.m.
7:30 a.m.	7:35 a.m.	7:40 a.m.	7:45 a.m.	7:50 a.m.
8:00 a.m.	8:05 a.m.	8:10 a.m.	8:15 a.m	8:20 a.m.

1. Suppose you catch the bus at 7:00 a.m. at Stop A.
   At what time will you get to Stop E? _____

2. Suppose you catch the bus at 7:40 a.m. at Stop C.
   At what time will you get to Stop A? _____

3. How long does it take the bus to travel from
   Stop E back to Stop A?  _____ minutes

4. Suppose you catch the bus at 8:15 a.m. at Stop D.
   At what time will you get to Stop B? _____

Name: _____

Daily Word Problems

WEEK 21 • DAY 1

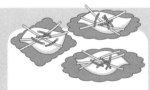

Tasty Creations

Chef Lorenzo made an appetizer called a Triple Crunchie by topping a cracker with shredded carrots, cucumbers, and garlic cream cheese. He used $\frac{7}{8}$ of a medium-sized carrot and $\frac{3}{4}$ of a medium-sized cucumber for 25 Triple Crunchies. How many carrots and cucumbers would he need to make 100 Triple Crunchies?

Work Space:

Answer:

_____ carrots and

_____ cucumbers

Name: _____

Daily Word Problems

WEEK 21 • DAY 2

Tasty Creations

Chef Lorenzo is known for his brightly colored dish that he calls Rainbow Spaghetti and Meat Blob. One serving has 379 calories.

If a family of six ordered the chef's famous spaghetti, how many calories would be in all six servings?

Work Space:

Answer:

_____ calories

Daily Word Problems

WEEK 21 • DAY 3

Tasty Creations

People love Chef Lorenzo's Triangle Tidbits. They are pastries with a surprise filling. People don't know what they will get until the food arrives!

The chef names the tidbits according to the triangle's sides and angles. Here is an Acute Equilateral Triangle Tidbit. Draw and name two other triangle tidbits the chef might make.

Work Space:

Answer:

_____

_____

Daily Word Problems

WEEK 21 • DAY 4

Tasty Creations

Chef Lorenzo wanted to test a new kind of soup at his restaurant. He calls it Freggie Soup because it has both fruits and vegetables in it.

The chef made $10\frac{1}{2}$ gallons of soup. By the end of the day, there were $2\frac{1}{8}$ gallons left. How many gallons of soup did people order that day?

Work Space:

Answer:

_____ gallons

Daily Word Problems

WEEK 21 • DAY 5

Tasty Creations

The graph shows how many people dined at Chef Lorenzo's restaurant during one week.

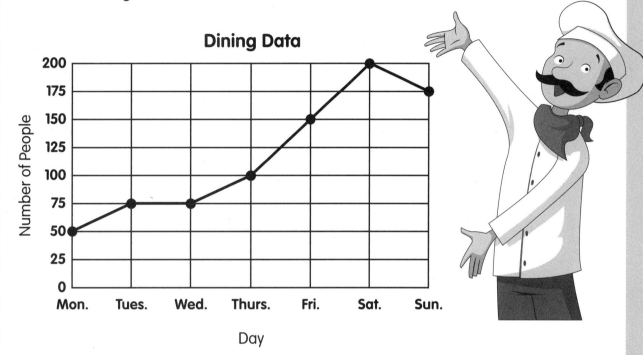

1. Which day had the fewest customers? _____

2. On which day did the restaurant have the most customers? _____

3. How many times greater is the highest number of customers than the lowest number of customers? _____ times greater

4. Chef Lorenzo always tests new dishes on Saturday to see how customers will like them. Is this a good idea? Why or why not?

_____

_____

_____

Daily Word Problems

WEEK 22 • DAY 1

School Garden

Work Space:

The students of Green Thumb Elementary started a school garden. Each class looked after a garden plot that had an area of 16 square feet.

If the school had 18 classes, what was the total area of the garden?

Answer:

_____ square feet

Daily Word Problems

WEEK 22 • DAY 2

School Garden

Work Space:

Mrs. Nguyen's students used $\frac{3}{8}$ of the garden space to plant beans and $\frac{1}{2}$ of the space to plant zucchini. They used the rest of the garden to plant green onions.

What fraction of the garden's total area was used for the green onions?

Answer:

_____ of the garden

Name: _____

Daily Word Problems

WEEK 22 • DAY 3

School Garden

Miss Olsen's class planted spinach, lettuce, and corn in their garden. They divided the space like this:

```
        2 ft
   ┌────┬────┐
   │ S  │ L  │ 2 ft
   ├────┴────┤
   │    C    │
   └─────────┘
      4 ft
```

The students are going to put fencing around the entire garden and between the three different plants. How many feet of fencing will they need?

Work Space:

Answer:

_____ feet

Name: _____

Daily Word Problems

WEEK 22 • DAY 4

School Garden

Mr. Kane's students wanted to plant tomatoes in $\frac{1}{2}$ of their garden space. They decided to plant cherry tomatoes in $\frac{3}{8}$ of the space reserved for tomatoes.

What fraction describes how much of the garden was used for cherry tomatoes?

Work Space:

Answer:

_____ of the garden

Daily Word Problems
WEEK 22 • DAY 5

School Garden

Mr. Garza's students measured the height of their bean plants each week for four weeks. They made a graph of their results.

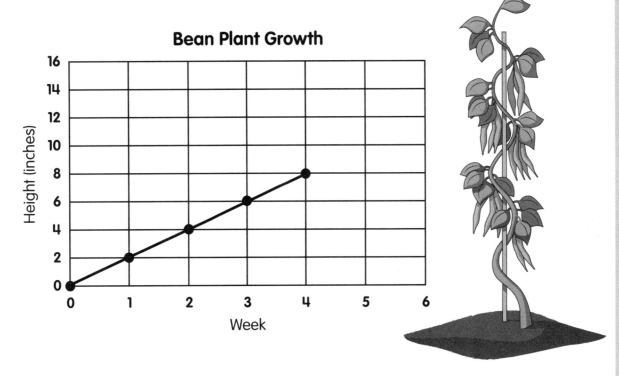

Bean Plant Growth

1. What pattern of growth do you see? _____

   _____

2. If the pattern continued, how tall would the plants be in Weeks 5 and 6?

   _____

3. Imagine that the plant's growth slows down after Week 6. How would this affect the line on the graph?

   _____

   _____

   _____

Daily Word Problems

WEEK 23 • DAY 1

Miniature Golf

Geeta played miniature golf at Putt-Putt Island Golf. There are 18 holes on the golf course. It took Geeta 4 strokes to sink the ball at every odd-numbered hole. She took 3 strokes at every even-numbered hole.

How many strokes did Geeta take on the whole course?

Work Space:

Answer:

_____ strokes

Daily Word Problems

WEEK 23 • DAY 2

Miniature Golf

In miniature golf, players hit the golf ball from the tee area to the hole. At Putt-Putt Island Golf, the first hole is 144 inches from the tee area. The second hole is 16 feet from the tee area. The third hole is 5 yards from the tee area.

Which hole is the farthest from the tee area?

Work Space:

Answer:

_____ hole

Daily Word Problems

WEEK 23 • DAY 3

Miniature Golf

Cerise played all 18 holes of miniature golf. She took 4 strokes at $\frac{1}{2}$ of the holes. She took 5 strokes at $\frac{1}{3}$ of the holes. She took 3 strokes at each of the remaining holes.

1. For what fraction of the holes did Cerise take 3 strokes?

2. What was Cerise's total number of strokes?

Work Space:

Answer:

1. _____ of the holes

2. _____ strokes

Daily Word Problems

WEEK 23 • DAY 4

Miniature Golf

Sheldon loves miniature golf. Last year, he played a total of 21,060 minutes at Putt-Putt Island Golf.

1. If Sheldon averaged 45 minutes per game, how many games did he play?

2. If he played the same number of games per week, how many games a week did he play? (Hint: A year has 52 weeks.)

Work Space:

Answer:

1. _____ games

2. _____ games per week

Daily Word Problems • EMC 3095 • © Evan-Moor Corporation

Daily Word Problems

WEEK 23 • DAY 5

Miniature Golf

The outdoor carpeting for the 16th hole at Putt-Putt Island Golf needs to be replaced. The cost of carpeting is $2.65 per square foot. Use the diagram to figure out how many square feet of carpeting are needed and what the cost will be.

9 ft

3 ft

9 ft

3 ft

1. How much carpeting is needed?   _____ ft²

2. How much will the carpeting cost? $_____

Daily Word Problems

WEEK 24 • DAY 1

Zany Experiments

Professor Zany loves experimenting! Today he placed small candies around the edge of a plate. He had $\frac{1}{6}$ cup of red candies, $\frac{1}{4}$ cup of yellow, and $\frac{1}{3}$ cup of blue. He poured hot water onto the middle of the plate and then watched. When the candies started dissolving, the colors mixed together to make beautiful swirls!

What was the total amount of candy Professor Zany used in his experiment?

Work Space:

Answer:

_____ cup

Daily Word Problems

WEEK 24 • DAY 2

Zany Experiments

Professor Zany filled two identical glass jars with water so that each had a water level of 10 cm. He left Jar A uncovered but covered Jar B with foil. Then he set the jars out in the sun.

Later, he checked the jars. The water level in Jar A was 6.8 cm, and the level in Jar B was 8.3 cm. How much did the water level drop in each jar? How much higher was the level in Jar B than in Jar A?

Work Space:

Answer:

Jar A's water level dropped _____ cm.

Jar B's water level dropped _____ cm.

The level in Jar B was _____ cm higher than in Jar A.

Daily Word Problems

WEEK 24 • DAY 3

Zany Experiments

Professor Zany had two cube-shaped boxes. Box A had sides that were 2 cm long. Cube B had sides that were 4 cm long. The professor said, "Since the second box has sides that are twice as long, its volume must be twice as great."

The professor started filling the boxes with centimeter cubes to check his theory. What did he find out?

Work Space:

Answer:

Cube A's volume: _____ cm^3

Cube B's volume: _____ cm^3

Cube B's volume was _____ times greater than Cube A's volume.

Daily Word Problems

WEEK 24 • DAY 4

Zany Experiments

Professor Zany slowly poured liquids into a jar. First, he poured in dark syrup. Then he added water, and finally, olive oil. Instead of mixing together, the liquids formed three separate layers!

Professor Zany measured the heights of the layers. The three together had a height of 7.5 cm. If all the layers were the same height, what was the height of each one?

Work Space:

Answer:

_____ cm

Daily Word Problems

WEEK 24 • DAY 5

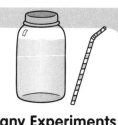

Zany Experiments

Professor Zany had a straw that was 20 cm long.
He gently blew through it and noticed it made a sound.
He wondered if the sound would change if he changed
the length of the straw. The professor decided to do
an experiment.

1. The professor cut off $\frac{1}{10}$ of the straw with scissors.

   How much did he cut off? _____ cm

   What was its length now? _____ cm

   When the professor blew through the straw, it made a higher sound
   than it did before!

2. The professor cut the straw two more times. Each time, he cut
   off $\frac{1}{10}$ of the remaining length. The professor blew through the
   straw to check the sound after every cut. Each time, the sound
   was higher than it was before.

   How much was cut off the second time? _____ cm

   How much was cut off the third time? _____ cm

   What was the length of the straw after the final cut? _____ cm

Daily Word Problems

WEEK 25 • DAY 1

Adventure Al

Al's friends call him Adventure Al because he loves activities that give him thrills and chills. One time, Al went bungee jumping off a cliff. He strapped an elastic bungee cord around his feet and then leaped 200 feet down. Wow! Then the cord bounced him back up to $\frac{6}{10}$ of the cliff's height before he fell down again.

How far did Al bounce back up after he jumped off the cliff?

Work Space:

Answer:

_____ feet

Daily Word Problems

WEEK 25 • DAY 2

Adventure Al

Adventure Al has made 2,000 skydiving jumps. Each time, he fell for 60 seconds before he opened his parachute.

What is the total number of hours Al has spent falling through the sky without an open parachute? Round your answer to the nearest whole hour.

Work Space:

Answer:

_____ hours

Daily Word Problems

WEEK 25 • DAY 3

Adventure Al

Name: _____

Adventure Al decided to check out the Greased Lightning Zip Line. He rode a jeep to the zip line site and took a chairlift to the top of the slope. He got fastened to the zip wire and then off he went, flying over hills and valleys!

Al traveled 5,202 feet in 60 seconds. That's almost a mile a minute! How many feet per second did he travel?

Work Space:

Answer:

_____ feet per second

Daily Word Problems

WEEK 25 • DAY 4

Adventure Al

Name: _____

Adventure Al and his pal Sal are riding in a bike race that winds through the mountains. Al checked his watch after 9 minutes. He had gone 4.8 km. Sal checked his watch after 4 minutes. He had gone 2.4 km. If they continued at their same speeds, who would be ahead in 15 minutes? Explain.

Work Space:

Answer:

_____

_____

_____

_____

Name: _____

Daily Word Problems

WEEK 25 • DAY 5

Adventure Al

Adventure Al went riding in a hot-air balloon. He boarded the balloon at 1:00 p.m. The graph shows how high he flew during his one-hour ride.

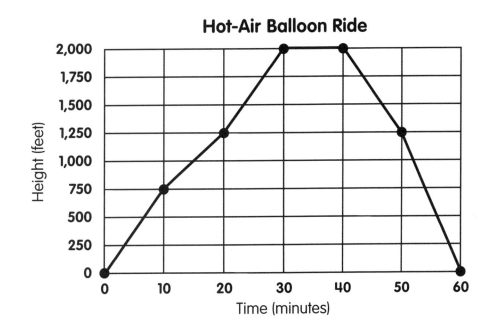

Hot-Air Balloon Ride

1. Find the point (10, 750) on the graph. What does it tell you about the balloon ride?

   _____

2. What was the balloon doing 25 minutes into the balloon ride?

   _____

3. At what time did the balloon reach its top height?   _____

4. At what time did the balloon start descending?   _____

5. Find the point (60, 0) on the graph. What does it tell you about the balloon ride?

   _____

Daily Word Problems

WEEK 26 • DAY 1

Hot-Air Balloons

Name: _____

There are 124 people waiting to take a ride in a hot-air balloon. The balloon can hold 14 passengers at one time.

1. The maximum number of people will ride in the balloon each time. How many rides will be needed for everyone to get a turn?

2. How many passengers will be in the balloon during the last ride?

Work Space:

Answer:

1. _____ rides

2. _____ passengers

Daily Word Problems

WEEK 26 • DAY 2

Hot-Air Balloons

Name: _____

During a hot-air balloon flight, Elise learned that she was flying 2,000 feet in the air. "We're really high!" she said.

"Not as high as the person who reached 68,986 feet," said the balloon operator. "That record was set in India in 2005."

Estimate how many times higher the world-record height was than the height reached during Elise's flight.

Work Space:

Answer:

about _____ times higher

Daily Word Problems • EMC 3095 • © Evan-Moor Corporation

Name: _____

Daily Word Problems

WEEK 26 • DAY 3

Hot-Air Balloons

At a hot-air balloon festival, 264 people showed up to watch the Friday evening liftoff. Saturday morning's liftoff drew 325 people. Sunday morning's event brought in twice as many people as the number who came Friday evening.

How many people came to watch the balloon liftoffs?

Work Space:

Answer:

_____ people

Name: _____

Daily Word Problems

WEEK 26 • DAY 4

Hot-Air Balloons

A hot-air balloon festival featured 240 colorful balloons. Most were the typical balloon shape, but $\frac{1}{3}$ of them were shaped like animals. One fourth of the animal-shaped balloons were popular cartoon characters.

1. How many balloons were cartoon characters?

2. What fraction of the total number of balloons were they?

Work Space:

Answer:

1. _____ balloons

2. _____ of the total number

Daily Word Problems

WEEK 26 • DAY 5

Hot-Air Balloons

The graph shows the number of adults and children who watched hot-air balloons lift off during one festival's five-day event.

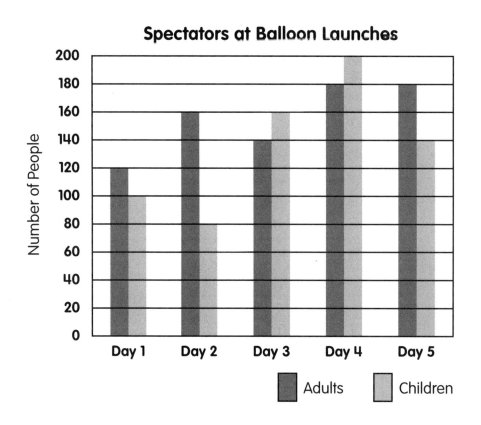

1. How many more adults were there than children on Day 1?   _____ more

2. On what day were there twice as many adults as children?   _____

3. On what days were there more children than adults?   _____

4. What is the range of the data for the adults? What is the range for children?
   (Hint: Range is the difference between the highest and lowest numbers.)

   Range for adults _____   Range for children _____

Name: _____

Daily Word Problems

WEEK 27 • DAY 1

Irene's Ice Cream

Irene owns an ice cream shop. It is open all year round. In April, Irene has 4 times as many customers as she does in January. In August, she has 3 times as many customers as she does in April.

Last August, Irene had 2,160 customers. How many did she have in January?

Work Space:

Answer:

_____ customers

Name: _____

Daily Word Problems

WEEK 27 • DAY 2

Irene's Ice Cream

At Irene's Ice Cream, a scoop of ice cream is 4 ounces. Last Tuesday, Irene went through 3 gallons of ice cream. How many scoops of ice cream did she serve? Use the chart to help you solve the problem.

8 ounces	=	1 cup
2 cups	=	1 pint
8 pints	=	1 gallon

Work Space:

Answer:

_____ scoops

Daily Word Problems

WEEK 27 • DAY 3

Irene's Ice Cream

Duwane's dad took the eight players on his basketball team to Irene's Ice Cream for ice cream sundaes.

Duwane's dad paid a total of $25.20 for the players' sundaes. How much did each one cost?

Work Space:

Answer:

$_____

Daily Word Problems

WEEK 27 • DAY 4

Irene's Ice Cream

Ubon and Lara each ordered a bowl of Butterscotch Swirl. Ubon sprinkled $2\frac{3}{4}$ ounces of chopped nuts on her ice cream. Lara put nuts on her ice cream, too, but she used only half the amount that Ubon did.

How many ounces of chopped nuts did Lara sprinkle on her ice cream?

Work Space:

Answer:

_____ ounces

Name: _____

Daily Word Problems

WEEK 27 • DAY 5

Irene's Ice Cream

Irene just enlarged her ice cream shop. The floor plan shows what the area looks like now.

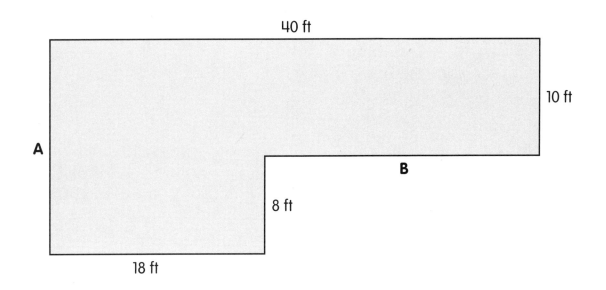

1. Irene noticed that the measurements for sides **A** and **B** were left off the plan. What are the missing measures?

   A _____ ft   **B** _____ ft

2. What is the perimeter of the remodeled shop?   _____ ft

3. What is the area of the remodeled shop?   _____ ft²

4. The shop's previous area was $\frac{3}{4}$ the size of the new one. What was the area of the shop before it was enlarged?   _____ ft²

Daily Word Problems

WEEK 28 • DAY 1

Let's Read!

Four friends compared how much time they spent reading yesterday. Piper read for only $\frac{1}{2}$ the amount of time that Mohini spent reading. Mohini read $\frac{2}{3}$ the amount of time that Arpie read. Arpie read twice as long as Lilah did.

Lilah read for $1\frac{1}{2}$ hours yesterday. For how long did Piper read?

Work Space:

Answer:

_____

Daily Word Problems

WEEK 28 • DAY 2

Let's Read!

Ashleigh loves reading about animals so much that she ordered a set of 10 wildlife books. When the books arrived, she placed them on her bookshelf like this:

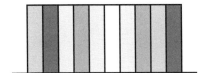

Each book was 1.5 cm wide. How wide was the row of 10 books?

Work Space:

Answer:

_____ cm

Name: _____

Daily Word Problems

WEEK 28 • DAY 3

Let's Read!

Diego and Inez read at home every day. For every 3 pages that Diego reads, Inez reads 5 pages.

Diego has just completed 18 pages. How many pages has Inez read?

Work Space:

Answer:

_____ pages

Name: _____

Daily Word Problems

WEEK 28 • DAY 4

Let's Read!

Kofi joined a book club. Each month, he gets 3 books in the mail. The books are shipped in a box that measures 2 inches by 8.5 inches by 11 inches.

What is the volume of the box?

Work Space:

Answer:

_____ cubic inches

Name: _____

Daily Word Problems

WEEK 28 • DAY 5

Let's Read!

Ms. Shay's and Mr. Ota's classes had a reading contest.
For one week, students kept track of the number of minutes they
read each night. The teachers then posted the results on a graph.

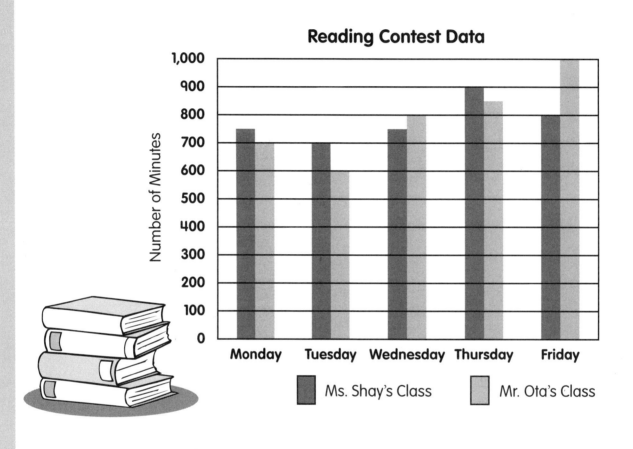

Reading Contest Data

1. On Monday, how many more minutes did Ms. Shay's
   class read than Mr. Ota's class? _____ more minutes

2. On Friday, how many more minutes did Mr. Ota's
   class read than Ms. Shay's class? _____ more minutes

3. Which class won the reading contest? _____

   How many more minutes did that class read? _____ more minutes

Name: _____

Daily Word Problems

WEEK 29 • DAY 1

Fairy Tale Chores

Little Red Riding Hood's grandmother asked her to bring 450 grams of cherries. The store's scale measured in milligrams, and the price was $10.00 per kilogram.

1. How many milligrams did she need?

2. How many kilograms is that?

3. How much did the cherries cost?

Work Space:

Answer:

1. _____ milligrams

2. _____ kilogram

3. $_____

Name: _____

Daily Word Problems

WEEK 29 • DAY 2

Fairy Tale Chores

Snow White was making a batch of biscuits for the Seven Dwarfs' lunches. Before she started, the flour bin had $8\frac{1}{4}$ cups of flour in it. After making the biscuits, the bin had $4\frac{3}{4}$ cups of flour left in it.

How much flour did Snow White use for the biscuits?

Work Space:

Answer:

_____ cups

Daily Word Problems

WEEK 29 • DAY 3

Fairy Tale Chores

Rapunzel was sitting in her tower and waiting for the prince to come for tea. She exclaimed, "He's coming in $15\frac{1}{2}$ minutes, so I had better hurry and tidy up!"

Rapunzel started cleaning and finished with 55 seconds to spare. How long did it take her to clean the room?

Work Space:

Answer:

_____ minutes _____ seconds

Daily Word Problems

WEEK 29 • DAY 4

Fairy Tale Chores

Cinderella has to wash the kitchen floor and the living room floor. The living room floor is 18 ft wide and 24 ft long. The kitchen floor is $\frac{2}{3}$ the width of the living room and $\frac{3}{4}$ of its length.

What is the area of the kitchen floor?

Work Space:

Answer:

_____ ft^2

Name: _____

Daily Word Problems
WEEK 29 • DAY 5

Fairy Tale Chores

Hansel and Gretel went into the woods to pick berries and chestnuts. They left a trail of breadcrumbs so they wouldn't get lost. The map shows where the two children went.

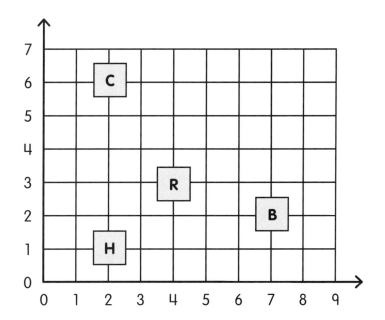

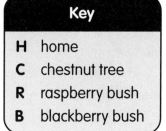

Key

H	home
C	chestnut tree
R	raspberry bush
B	blackberry bush

1. Write an ordered pair for each location. The first one has been done for you.

   home   ___(2, 1)___   raspberry bush   _____

   chestnut tree _____   blackberry bush   _____

2. Hansel and Gretel were careful not to go near the witch's gingerbread house. It is located at (8, 6). Draw a point on the map at that location and label it **W**.

3. A pine tree is halfway between the chestnut tree and the witch's house. Draw a point on the map showing its location and label it **P**.

   Write an ordered pair describing the location. _____

Daily Word Problems

WEEK 30 • DAY 1

Fire Stations

Work Space:

Fire Station A stays really busy. It receives 1,200 calls a year!

1. How many calls does the fire station average each month?

2. How many calls does it average a day? Round your answer to the nearest whole number.

Answer:

1. _____ calls a month

2. _____ calls a day

Daily Word Problems

WEEK 30 • DAY 2

Fire Stations

Work Space:

The fire hoses at Station A are each 30 yards long. The firefighters connect the hoses to make them long enough to reach any house from a fire hydrant.

How many hoses would the firefighters need to connect in order to reach a house that is 220 feet from the fire hydrant?

Answer:

_____ hoses

Name: _____

Daily Word Problems

WEEK 30 • DAY 3

Fire Stations

In a recent timed drill, it took firefighters 10.5 seconds to reach the fire pole, 11.5 seconds to slide down the pole, 18.6 seconds to put on their gear, and 12.7 seconds to climb aboard the fire truck.

How long did it take the firefighters to get ready and board the fire truck?

Work Space:

Answer:

_____

Name: _____

Daily Word Problems

WEEK 30 • DAY 4

Fire Stations

In one city, there is 1 fire station for every 10,000 homes.

1. If there are 121,000 homes, how many fire stations would you expect in the city?

2. If there were 15 firefighters assigned to each station, how many firefighters would be working for the city?

Work Space:

Answer:

1. _____ fire stations

2. _____ firefighters

Name: _____

Daily Word Problems

WEEK 30 • DAY 5

Fire Stations

The grid represents the map of a town. Each rectangle represents a city block. The **R**s represent blocks of residential homes.

There are four fire stations in the town. The **1** on the grid represents Fire Station #1. Use the clues below to determine the locations of the other three fire stations. Then write **2**, **3**, and **4** in the correct spaces.

	R		R		R	R		R	
	R	R	R			R			R
R		**1**	R				R		R
R		R			R				R
R	R								R
R		R		R			R		R
	R							R	
R	R		R	R		R	R	R	R

Clues:

- No fire stations are located along the perimeter of the city.
- You can go 4 blocks south from Fire Station #1 and arrive at Fire Station #4.
- You can go 6 blocks west from Fire Station #2 and arrive at another fire station.
- If you go 3 blocks north from Fire Station #3 and then 2 blocks east, you will reach another fire station.

Daily Word Problems • EMC 3095 • © Evan-Moor Corporation

Name: _____

Daily Word Problems

WEEK 31 • DAY 1

At the **Movies**

A movie theater was showing four movies: *Superhero Zero, Spy Guy Returns, Dancing Days,* and *My Little Kitties.* Last Friday, $\frac{1}{2}$ of the people who bought tickets went to see the superhero movie, $\frac{2}{9}$ went to see the spy thriller, and $\frac{1}{6}$ went to see the musical.

What fraction of the people went to see the animated film about kittens?

Work Space:

Answer:

_____ of the people

Name: _____

Daily Word Problems

WEEK 31 • DAY 2

At the **Movies**

Mandy belongs to a movie theater club. Every time she sees a movie at the club theater, she earns 150 points toward the price of a ticket. Once she earns 1,800 points, she receives a free movie ticket.

Mandy has gone to the movies 7 times. How many more times does she need to go in order to get a free ticket?

Work Space:

Answer:

_____ more times

Name: _____

Daily Word Problems

WEEK 31 • DAY 3

At the **Movies**

Keith saw that there were 12 rows of 20 seats in the movie theater. He also saw that every 5th seat was empty.

1. How many seats in the theater were empty?

2. What fraction of the theater was filled?

Work Space:

Answer:

1. _____ seats

2. _____ of the theater

Name: _____

Daily Word Problems

WEEK 31 • DAY 4

At the **Movies**

The movie *Chipmunks to the Rescue* is popular with preschoolers. At one showing, $\frac{2}{3}$ of the audience was made up of children under 5. Of that group, $\frac{2}{5}$ brought toy chipmunks with them.

1. What fraction of the audience was young children with toy chipmunks?

2. If there were 150 people in the audience, how many were young children with toy chipmunks?

Work Space:

Answer:

1. _____ of the audience

2. _____ young children

   Daily Word Problems • EMC 3095 • © Evan-Moor Corporation

Name: _____

Daily Word Problems
WEEK 31 • DAY 5

At the **Movies**

The Movie Magic Theater House shows movies 24 hours a day! A new movie starts every 2 hours and 20 minutes. The theater continuously plays one movie after another. The only exception is a 40-minute break that occurs after the 11:00 p.m. showing.

1. The movie *Gorilla Party* started at 10:00 a.m. At what time did the next movie start?

_____

2. A group of friends came to a 4:00 p.m. showing. They watched three movies in a row. At what time did they leave the theater?

_____

3. The movie *Superhero Zero* was so popular that the theater played it in every time slot last Saturday. How many times was the movie shown that day?

_____ times

Daily Word Problems

WEEK 32 • DAY 1

Breakfast Math

Svetlana loves cereal so much that her dad buys a box just for her! Two days ago, the box was $\frac{5}{6}$ full. Now the box is only $\frac{3}{8}$ full.

How much of the box of cereal did Svetlana eat in the last two days?

Work Space:

Answer:

_____ of the box

Daily Word Problems

WEEK 32 • DAY 2

Breakfast Math

Connor bought a half-gallon carton of orange juice. He and his sister each drink 8 ounces of orange juice every morning.

If Connor and his sister are the only ones who drink the orange juice, how many days will the carton last?

8 ounces	=	1 cup
2 cups	=	1 pint
8 pints	=	1 gallon

Work Space:

Answer:

_____ days

Name: _____

Daily Word Problems

WEEK 32 • DAY 3

Breakfast Math

The Breakfast Place serves many different dishes using eggs. Each dish is made with 2 eggs. Last month, the restaurant served 483 omelets, 312 scrambled egg dishes, and 195 poached egg dishes.

How many dozen eggs did the restaurant use last month?

Work Space:

Answer:

_____ dozen eggs

Name: _____

Daily Word Problems

WEEK 32 • DAY 4

Breakfast Math

Mei eats half a grapefruit for breakfast 5 days a week before school. Juan eats a whole grapefruit each weekend morning.

Who would eat more grapefruits in February? How many more would that person eat?

Work Space:

Answer:

_____ would eat

_____ more grapefruits.

Name: _____

Daily Word Problems
WEEK 32 • DAY 5

Breakfast Math

Children who are 9 years old and older need 1,300 milligrams of calcium every day. Here are some breakfast foods they can get their calcium from:

Food	Serving Size	Calcium (mg)
milk	1 cup	300
yogurt	$\frac{1}{2}$ cup	150
egg	1 large	28
orange	1	50
banana	1	6
bread	1 slice	32

Read what the following children ate for breakfast. Then write how many more milligrams of calcium they'll need to eat during the day.

1. Matthew – 1 cup of milk
   $\frac{1}{2}$ orange
   2 bananas
   $\frac{1}{2}$ cup of yogurt

   Matthew needs _____ more milligrams of calcium.

2. Elsa – 1 cup of milk
   1 egg
   1 slice of bread

   Elsa needs _____ more milligrams of calcium.

Daily Word Problems • EMC 3095 • © Evan-Moor Corporation

Daily Word Problems

WEEK 33 • DAY 1

Earn, Save, Spend

Sierra has been saving money for the summer. During the first five months of the year, she saved $45 a month. In June, she saved $45, but then she spent $\frac{1}{3}$ of it for her mom's birthday.

How much money did Sierra save for the summer?

Work Space:

Answer:

$_____

Daily Word Problems

WEEK 33 • DAY 2

Earn, Save, Spend

Antonio is earning money by painting both sides of the fence along the side of his house. The fence is 15 yards long and 2 yards tall. His parents will pay $0.25 for every square foot of fencing that he paints.

How much money will Antonio earn by painting the fence?

Work Space:

Answer:

$_____

Daily Word Problems

WEEK 33 • DAY 3

Earn, Save, Spend

Badia has been saving money for an upcoming trip. She has earned a total of $181 made up of 20-dollar, 10-dollar, 5-dollar, and 1-dollar bills.

Badia has the same number of tens as ones. She has half as many fives as ones. The number of twenties is 1 less than the number of tens. How many of each bill does Badia have?

Work Space:

Answer:

_____ twenties, _____ tens,

_____ fives, _____ ones

Daily Word Problems

WEEK 33 • DAY 4

Earn, Save, Spend

Last year, Isabel saved $328.40 from babysitting. She spent $\frac{1}{10}$ of the money on a mini-backpack.

1. How much money did Isabel spend?

2. How much money did she have left?

Work Space:

Answer:

1. $_____

2. $_____

Daily Word Problems

WEEK 33 • DAY 5

Earn, Save, Spend

Mason earns money by doing chores for his neighbors.
Read below to find out how much money he makes.

1. Mason takes out the trash for
   Mrs. Odipo twice a week. He gets
   paid $0.75 each time. How much
   does he get paid a week?

   $_____

2. Mason mows the lawn once a week for Mr. Chang. He gets paid
   $5.50 each time. How much does he get paid after 2 weeks?

   $_____

3. Mr. Constantine pays Mason $8.25 to weed and water his garden
   every week. How much does he get paid after 4 weeks?

   $_____

4. Miss Washuta pays Mason $4.00 to wash her car every 2 weeks.
   How much does he get paid after 6 weeks?

   $_____

5. Mason wants to save $100.00 for a new bike. How many weeks
   will it take him to earn the money?

   _____ weeks

Name: _____

Daily Word Problems

WEEK 34 • DAY 1

Woodworks

Taylor creates sculptures by gluing 1-inch wooden cubes together to make statues, towers, and other interesting shapes. He stores the cubes in a box that is 12 inches wide, 12 inches tall, and 20 inches long.

How many cubes will fill the box?

Work Space:

Answer:

_____ cubes

Name: _____

Daily Word Problems

WEEK 34 • DAY 2

Woodworks

Dana likes to make colorful toy cars out of wood. Each car weighs 140 grams. Dana has made 15 cars so far.

1. What is the total weight of the cars she has made?

2. What is the weight in kilograms?

Work Space:

Answer:

1. _____ grams

2. _____ kilograms

Daily Word Problems

WEEK 34 • DAY 3

Woodworks

Haunani builds wooden tables. Every tabletop she makes is a polygon with sides of equal length. Haunani made three tables shaped like this:

The perimeter of each table is 126 inches. What are the side lengths of each table?

Work Space:

Answer:

triangular table _____ in.

square table _____ in.

hexagonal table _____ in.

Daily Word Problems

WEEK 34 • DAY 4

Woodworks

Luis made the letter **L** in his woodworking class. It looks like this:

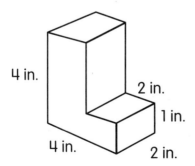

4 in.

2 in.

1 in.

4 in.

2 in.

What is the volume of the figure?

Work Space:

Answer:

_____ in.³

Daily Word Problems

WEEK 34 • DAY 5

Woodworks

Nevine stacked 5 rows of wooden tiles to make this design:

1. What will the 6th and 7th rows look like?
   Draw the shapes on the picture.

2. What kind of shapes are in the 6th row,
   and how many are there?

   _____

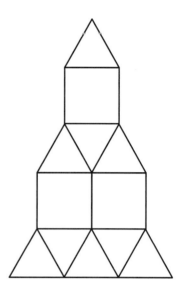

3. What kind of shapes are in the 7th row,
   and how many are there?

   _____

4. Without drawing the shapes, describe what the 18th
   and 19th rows will look like. Explain how you know.

   _____

   _____

   _____

   _____

   _____

Name: _____

Daily Word Problems

Summer Camp

WEEK 35 • DAY 1

Camp Wachoo is located on a large piece of land that measures 1,400 acres.

There are 640 acres in one square mile. Estimate the area in square miles.

Work Space:

Answer:

_____ square miles

Name: _____

Daily Word Problems

Summer Camp

WEEK 35 • DAY 2

There were 40 cars dropping off kids at Camp Wachoo. One half of the cars were white. Then 10 of the white cars left.

What fraction of the remaining cars were white?

Work Space:

Answer:

_____

Daily Word Problems

WEEK 35 • DAY 3

Summer Camp

The crafts leader was preparing materials for a woodworking project. She took a 3-foot length of wood. Then she cut the wood into pieces that were 4.5 inches long.

1. How many pieces did she get?

2. If each of the 70 campers needed 1 piece, how many 3-foot lengths of wood would she need to cut?

Work Space:

Answer:

1. _____ pieces

2. _____ lengths of wood

Daily Word Problems

WEEK 35 • DAY 4

Summer Camp

A group of campers went hiking at 9:00 a.m. to Hightop Ridge. It took them 45 minutes to reach the area. After spending half an hour there, they hiked back to their campsite. It only took 35 minutes for the campers to go back because they were going downhill.

At what time did the group return to the campsite?

Work Space:

Answer:

_____

Daily Word Problems

WEEK 35 • DAY 5

Summer Camp

The map shows Camp Wachoo and its surrounding area.

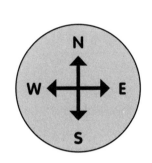

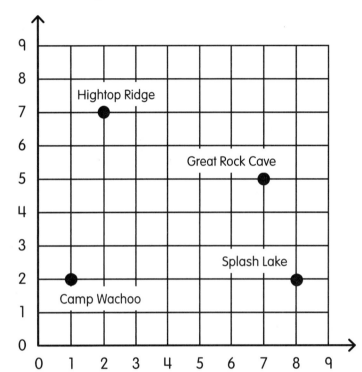

1. What ordered pairs describe the following locations?

    Camp Wachoo _____   Great Rock Cave _____

    Hightop Ridge _____   Splash Lake _____

2. If each unit on the grid represents $\frac{1}{4}$ mile, how far away
    is Splash Lake from the campsite? _____ miles

3. Suppose you can walk only in a north, south, east, or west direction.
    Explain how you could get from the campsite to Great Rock Cave.

    _____

    _____

    _____

Name: _____

Daily Word Problems

WEEK 36 • DAY 1

Travel Tales

There were 156 people waiting to get on a plane. Every 4th person was wearing blue pants. Every 6th person was wearing sneakers. Every 8th person was wearing glasses.

How many people were wearing blue pants, sneakers, and glasses?

Work Space:

Answer:

_____ people

Name: _____

Daily Word Problems

WEEK 36 • DAY 2

Travel Tales

Josh was waiting at the airport to leave on his vacation when a heavy storm came through. Three fourths of the flights were canceled that day, including Josh's.

There were 396 flights scheduled that day. How many planes were able to leave the airport?

Work Space:

Answer:

_____ planes

Daily Word Problems • EMC 3095 • © Evan-Moor Corporation

Name: _____

Daily Word Problems

Travel Tales

WEEK 36 • DAY 3

Nigel went on a trip and bought 12 boxes of tea for his friends. Each box was a 3-inch cube. Nigel packed the boxes into a larger box like this:

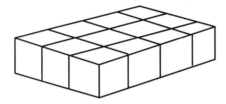

What was the volume of the larger box?

Work Space:

Answer:

_____ in.^{3}

Name: _____

Daily Word Problems

Travel Tales

WEEK 36 • DAY 4

Erin is going to visit Iti Island with her family. The point (1, 0) on the grid shows where the airport is located. The island is 3 units north and 3 units east of the airport.

What ordered pair gives the location of the island?

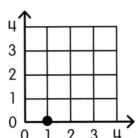

Work Space:

Answer:

_____

Daily Word Problems

WEEK 36 • DAY 5

Travel Tales

Erin and her family took a trip to Iti Island and bought souvenirs. Read the clues and fill in the chart to determine what each person bought. When you know that a name and an item **don't** go together, make an **X** under that item and across from that name. When you know that a name and an item **do** go together, write **YES** in that box.

Clues:

- Erin and Ellie did not buy a mug or a T-shirt.
- Dad did not buy a cap or sunglasses.
- Ethan and Ellie did not buy a keychain or sunglasses.
- Mom bought a mug or a T-shirt.
- Ethan bought something to wear.

	cap	keychain	mug	sunglasses	T-shirt
Mom					
Dad					
Erin					
Ethan					
Ellie					

Write the name of each souvenir beside the correct name.

Mom _____

Dad _____

Erin _____

Ethan _____

Ellie _____

Answer Key

Week 1

Day 1: 14 students

Day 2: Jin's lessons – 50 minutes
Micah's lessons –
40 minutes

Day 3: 1. 5 ft wide and 2 ft deep
2. 10 ft²

Day 4: 1,232 keys

Day 5: 1. 57 seats
2. about 440 seats
Example: The first 10
rows have 30, 33, 36,
39, 42, 45, 48, 51, 54,
57 seats. If you round
each number to the
nearest 10, you get
two 30s, three 40s,
four 50s, and one 60.
That makes
60 + 120 + 200 + 60 =
440 seats.

Week 2

Day 1: Corky – 22 pounds
Muffin – 11 pounds
Rufus – 44 pounds

Day 2: 60 fish

Day 3: Casey – 2 cats
Dylan – 2 dogs
Hannah – 4 hamsters
Gabi – 12 goldfish

Day 4: Example: Yes. The 2 x 2
pieces are 4 ft² each. The
2 x 3 pieces are 6 ft² each.
The total area is 32 ft², the
same as the plywood sheet.

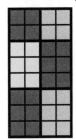

Day 5: 1. 5 ft
2. 5 ft
3. 44 ft
4. 87 ft²

Week 3

Day 1: Trent – 6:44 a.m.
Jehna – 6:52 a.m.
Matt – 6:55 a.m.

Day 2: 768 feet

Day 3: 324 chocolates

Day 4: Nutty Chews – 1,025 boxes
Creamy Caramels –
2,050 boxes

Day 5: 1. February; $80,000
2. $50,000
3. Example: They started
out in the middle and
basically went down
a little each month. July
went a little lower than
usual.

Week 4

Day 1: Examples: All of the
polygon's angles have
the same measure. The
number of sides equals
the number of angles. The
shapes are symmetrical.

Day 2: 75 minutes; 1¼ hours

Day 3: 5¼ cups

Day 4: 1. 1¾ OR 1½ hours
2. 6¼ hours

Day 5: Math – 60 minutes
Reading – 60 minutes
Writing – 40 minutes
History – 40 minutes
Science – 40 minutes;

Possible explanation:
Math and Reading each
take up one-fourth of the
circle. One-fourth of 240
is 60. Writing, History, and
Science each take up one-
sixth of the circle. One-
sixth of 240 is 40.

Week 5

Day 1: 4 toy stores

Day 2: $21.12

Day 3: 2 pennies, 2 nickels,
3 dimes, 5 quarters

Day 4: 128 feet

Day 5: 1. 27 pairs
2. 8½
3. 8 pairs, 11 pairs
4. 3 pairs

Week 6

Day 1: 1. 270 students
2. 90 students

Day 2: length: 50 yards
width: 25 yards

Day 3: 31.5 pounds

Day 4: 50 ice cream cones

Day 5: 1. 47 students
2. 4th graders
3. 3rd grade
4. 5th grade
5. Both groups have the
same number.

Week 7

Day 1: 1,093 patents

Day 2: 986.5 more hours

Day 3: 23 years old

Day 4: 500 dolls

Day 5: 1. 25 films
2. 4 minutes
3. 300 times

Week 8

Day 1: 10.2 miles

Day 2: 1. 12.05 cm
2. 1,205 cm

Day 3: 1½ gallons

Day 4: 7 cuts, 8 pieces;
Look at the number of
sides in the shape. The
number of cuts is 3 less
and the number of pieces
is 2 less.

Day 5:

4 H	5 D 8 D
	7 H 10 H
2 S 3 C	9 C
6 S	

Criteria and groupings
will vary. Examples: even
number, odd number,
less than 6, greater than 5.

Week 9

Day 1: trapezoid

Day 2: 240 children

Day 3: 4 times

Day 4: 1. 105 tickets
2. Buy 5 packs of 20 for $25. Buy 5 individual tickets for $2. Total cost: $27

Day 5: 1. The increase in riders goes up 10 more each day.
2. 310 riders
3. Sunday, 420 riders

Week 10

Day 1: 12,000 rides

Day 2: 1. 2,853 feet longer
2. It is greater than half a mile. Half a mile is about 2,600 feet, so 2,800 is greater.

Day 3: 40 times greater

Day 4: about 1,500 feet shorter Example: I rounded the lengths to 3,000 and 4,500 before subtracting.

Day 5: 1. 29 years
2. Twisted Colossus, 2,400 feet longer
3. 16 minutes, 12 seconds

Week 11

Day 1: about 410 books (100 + 130 + 90 + 90)

Day 2: 2.3 cm

Day 3: $536.25

Day 4: 5 feet 5 inches

Day 5: Example:

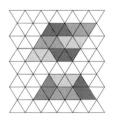

Week 12

Day 1: $8.80

Day 2: 4 dogs

Day 3: 6 small dogs, 6 large dogs

Day 4: 1. 2 ¼ miles
2. 8 dogs

Day 5: 1. 1/2
2. 1/5
3. 2/6 OR 1/3
4. 5/20 OR 1/4
5. 2/20 OR 1/10

Week 13

Day 1: Zip – 71 laps
Dash – 71 laps
Boomer – 77 laps

Day 2: third race – 235 miles
fourth race – 235 miles

Day 3: 8.4 seconds

Day 4: 10 races

Day 5: 1st – Dash
2nd – Ace
3rd – Boomer
4th – Miles
5th – Zip

Week 14

Day 1: 1. $0.25
2. 5 more game tokens

Day 2: 380,350

Day 3: $12.40

Day 4: 2,250 points

Day 5: 1. H
2. C
3. O

Week 15

Day 1: 17 loads

Day 2: laundry soap – $6.30
fabric softener – $3.15

Day 3: He will need to pull out 4 socks. The first 3 could be different colors (yellow, blue, black). The 4th one will have to match a color he already pulled out.

Day 4: 22 feet 8 ¼ inches

Day 5: 1. 432 loads
2. $756
3. $43.20 more

Week 16

Day 1: 1. 2,400 kilometers
2. 144,000 kilometers

Day 2: 45 tourists

Day 3: 1. 7/16
2. Laser Falls

Day 4: There were more yellow Zingalings. 3/5 of the herd was yellow, so that's more than half.

Day 5: Table should show the following measures:

5 cm	20 cm
10 cm	40 cm
15 cm	60 cm
20 cm	80 cm

1. The flower's perimeter is 4 times greater than the center's perimeter.
2. 125 cm, 500 cm

Week 17

Day 1: 3/5 of a pizza Drawings should show 3 pizzas with each one divided into fifths.

Day 2: $6.76

Day 3: 3 blocks of cheese

Day 4: 1. less than 1 inch
2. 1/8 inch less

Day 5: cheese only – 4
pepperoni only – 4
mushroom and sausage – 2
ham and pineapple – 3
mushroom and olive – 1
hamburger – 1
bacon and onion – 1

Week 18

Day 1: 1,710 pounds

Day 2: $234.00

Day 3: 5,403 pounds

Day 4: 2,296 tubes

Day 5: 1. 2 pounds
2. 1½ pounds
3. 6 classes
4. 15 ¾ pounds

Week 19

Day 1: 17 hours

Day 2: 36 people

Day 3: 9:35 a.m.

Day 4: $32.50

Day 5: 1. 12 people
2. 6 people
3. 6 more
4. 13/52 OR 1/4
   13/52 OR 1/4
   20/52 OR 5/13
   6/52 OR 3/26

Week 20

Day 1: 1. 108 feet
2. 1,296 inches

Day 2: 1,974 people

Day 3: $33.00

Day 4: 4 times

Day 5: 1. 7:20 a.m.
2. 8:00 a.m.
3. 10 minutes
4. 8:35 a.m.

Week 21

Day 1: 3 ½ carrots and
3 cucumbers

Day 2: 2,274 calories

Day 3: Drawings will vary, but
they should match the
names given. Examples:
Right Scalene Triangle
Tidbit, Obtuse Isosceles
Triangle Tidbit

Day 4: 8 ⅜ gallons

Day 5: 1. Monday
2. Saturday
3. 4 times greater
4. Example: It's a good idea.
   More people are at the
   restaurant then to give
   the chef feedback on
   the food.

Week 22

Day 1: 288 square feet

Day 2: 1/8 of the garden

Day 3: 22 feet

Day 4: 3/16 of the garden

Day 5: 1. The plants grow
   2 inches every week.
2. Week 5 – 10 inches,
   Week 6 – 12 inches
3. It would be flatter/less
   steep.

Week 23

Day 1: 63 strokes

Day 2: second hole

Day 3: 1. 1/6 of the holes
2. 75 strokes

Day 4: 1. 468 games
2. 9 games per week

Day 5: 1. 45 ft²
2. $119.25

Week 24

Day 1: 9/12 OR 3/4 cup

Day 2: 3.2 cm, 1.7 cm, 1.5 cm

Day 3: Cube A's volume: 8 cm³
Cube B's volume: 64 cm³;
8 times greater

Day 4: 2.5 cm

Day 5: 1. 2 cm, 18 cm
2. 1.8 cm, 1.62 cm, 14.58 cm

Week 25

Day 1: 120 feet

Day 2: 33 hours

Day 3: 86.7 feet per second

Day 4: Sal would be ahead.
Sal can ride 4.8 km in
8 minutes, which is one
minute faster than Al can.

Day 5: 1. After 10 minutes, the
   balloon was 750 feet
   in the air.
2. It was still climbing
   higher. OR It was about
   1,625 feet in the air.
3. 1:30 p.m.
4. 1:40 p.m.
5. The balloon landed
   60 minutes after the
   trip started.

Week 26

Day 1: 1. 9 rides
2. 12 passengers

Day 2: about 35 times higher

Day 3: 1,117 people

Day 4: 1. 20 balloons
2. 1/12 of the total number

Day 5: 1. 20 more
2. Day 2
3. Days 3 and 4
4. Range for adults – 60
   Range for children – 120

Week 27

Day 1: 180 customers

Day 2: 96 scoops

Day 3: $3.15

Day 4: 1⅜ ounces

Day 5: 1. A – 18 ft, B – 22 ft
2. 116 ft
3. 544 ft²
4. 408 ft²

Week 28

Day 1: 1 hour

Day 2: 15 cm

Day 3: 30 pages

Day 4: 187 cubic inches

Day 5: 1. 50 more minutes
2. 200 more minutes
3. Mr. Ota's class,
   50 more minutes

Week 29

Day 1: 1. 450,000 mg
2. 0.45 kg
3. $4.50

Day 2: 3 ½ cups

Day 3: 14 minutes 35 seconds

Day 4: 216 ft²

Day 5: 1. chestnut tree (2, 6)
   raspberry bush (4, 3)
   blackberry bush (7, 2)
2. A point should be
   placed at (8, 6) and
   labeled W.
3. A point should be
   placed at (5, 6) and
   labeled P.

Week 30

Day 1: 1. 100 calls a month
2. 3 calls a day

Day 2: 3 hoses

Day 3: 53.3 seconds

Day 4: 1. 12 fire stations
2. 180 firefighters

Day 5:

Week 31

Day 1: 1/9 of the people

Day 2: 5 more times

Day 3: 1. 48 seats
        2. 4/5 of the theater

Day 4: 1. 4/15 of the audience
        2. 40 young children

Day 5: 1. 12:20 p.m.
        2. 11:00 p.m.
        3. 10 times

Week 32

Day 1: 11/24 of the box

Day 2: 4 days

Day 3: 165 dozen eggs

Day 4: Mei would eat 2 more
        grapefruits.

Day 5: Matthew – 813 more
        milligrams

        Elsa – 940 more
        milligrams

Week 33

Day 1: $255

Day 2: $135.00

Day 3: 5 twenties, 6 tens, 3 fives,
        6 ones

Day 4: 1. $32.84
        2. $295.56

Day 5: 1. $1.50
        2. $11.00
        3. $33.00
        4. $12.00
        5. 6 weeks

Week 34

Day 1: 2,880 cubes

Day 2: 1. 2,100 grams
        2. 2.1 kilograms

Day 3: triangular table – 42 in.
        square table – 31.5 in.
        hexagonal table – 21 in.

Day 4: 20 in.³

Day 5: 1.

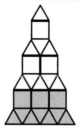

2. 3 squares
3. 7 equilateral triangles
4. 18th row – 9 squares;
   Even-numbered rows
   have squares. The
   number of squares
   is half the row number.

   19th row – 19 equilateral
   triangles; Odd-numbered
   rows have triangles. The
   number of triangles is
   the same as the row
   number.

Week 35

Day 1: 2 square miles

Day 2: 1/3

Day 3: 1. 8 pieces
        2. 9 lengths of wood

Day 4: 10:50 a.m.

Day 5: 1. Camp Wachoo (1, 2)
           Hightop Ridge (2, 7)
           Great Rock Cave (7, 5)
           Splash Lake (8, 2)
        2. 1¾ miles
        3. Example: Walk north
           ¾ miles. Then go east
           1½ miles.

Week 36

Day 1: 6 people

Day 2: 99 planes

Day 3: 324 in.³

Day 4: (4, 3)

Day 5: Mom – mug
        Dad – keychain
        Erin – sunglasses
        Ethan – T-shirt
        Ellie – cap

Day-by-Day Skills List

Week 1

Day	Skills
1	Division
2	Fractions—multiplication and division; Time
3	Perimeter and area
4	Multiplication
5	Addition and subtraction; Estimation; Patterns

Week 2

Day	Skills
1	Addition and subtraction; Multiplication
2	Addition and subtraction; Fractions—multiplication and division; Logical thinking
3	Addition and subtraction; Multiplication; Logical thinking
4	Perimeter and area; Geometry
5	Perimeter and area

Week 3

Day	Skills
1	Time
2	Fractions—multiplication and division; Perimeter and area
3	Multiplication
4	Multiplication; Fractions—multiplication and division; Logical thinking
5	Addition and subtraction; Graphs, charts, and maps

Week 4

Day	Skills
1	Geometry
2	Time
3	Fractions—addition and subtraction; Weight and capacity
4	Fractions—addition and subtraction; Time; Patterns
5	Division; Fractions—multiplication and division; Graphs, charts, and maps

Week 5

Day	Skills
1	Division; Logical thinking
2	Fractions—multiplication and division; Decimals—addition and subtraction
3	Decimals—addition and subtraction; Logical thinking
4	Addition and subtraction; Linear measurement
5	Graphs, charts, and maps

Week 6

Day	Skills
1	Fractions—multiplication and division
2	Addition and subtraction; Perimeter and area; Logical thinking
3	Decimals—place value; Weight and capacity
4	Addition and subtraction; Multiplication; Time
5	Addition and subtraction; Graphs, charts, and maps

Week 7

Day	Skills
1	Decimals—place value
2	Decimals—addition and subtraction
3	Addition and subtraction
4	Division; Fractions—multiplication and division
5	Multiplication; Division; Time

Week 8

Day	Skills
1	Decimals—addition and subtraction; Linear measurement
2	Decimals—place value; Linear measurement
3	Weight and capacity
4	Geometry; Patterns
5	Logical thinking

Week 9

Day	Skills
1	Geometry
2	Multiplication; Division; Time
3	Division
4	Addition and subtraction; Multiplication; Decimals—multiplication
5	Addition and subtraction; Graphs, charts, and maps; Patterns

Week 10

Day	Skills
1	Division
2	Addition and subtraction; Estimation; Linear measurement
3	Decimals—division
4	Addition and subtraction; Estimation
5	Addition and subtraction; Time; Graphs, charts, and maps

Week 11

Day	Skills
1	Addition and subtraction; Estimation
2	Decimals—addition and subtraction; Decimals—multiplication; Linear measurement
3	Division; Decimals—addition and subtraction; Decimals—multiplication
4	Addition and subtraction; Linear measurement
5	Geometry

Week 12

Day	Skills
1	Decimals—multiplication
2	Time
3	Addition and subtraction; Multiplication
4	Fractions—multiplication and division; Linear measurement
5	Fractions—identification and comparison; Graphs, charts, and maps

Daily Word Problems • EMC 3095 • © Evan-Moor Corporation

Week 13

Day	Skills
1	Logical thinking
2	Logical thinking
3	Decimals—addition and subtraction
4	Decimals—place value; Decimals—addition and subtraction; Decimals—division
5	Logical thinking

Week 14

Day	Skills
1	Decimals—addition and subtraction; Decimals—division
2	Addition and subtraction; Division
3	Decimals—addition and subtraction
4	Multiplication
5	Coordinate plane; Graphs, charts, and maps; Logical thinking

Week 15

Day	Skills
1	Division
2	Decimals—addition and subtraction; Decimals—division
3	Logical thinking
4	Fractions—addition and subtraction; Linear measurement
5	Multiplication; Decimals—addition and subtraction; Decimals—multiplication

Week 16

Day	Skills
1	Multiplication; Time
2	Division
3	Fractions—addition and subtraction; Fractions—identification and comparison
4	Fractions—identification and comparison
5	Perimeter and area; Geometry; Patterns

Week 17

Day	Skills
1	Fractions—multiplication and division
2	Decimals—addition and subtraction
3	Estimation; Decimals—addition and subtraction; Weight and capacity; Graphs, charts, and maps
4	Fractions—addition and subtraction
5	Addition and subtraction; Fractions—multiplication and division

Week 18

Day	Skills
1	Addition and subtraction; Multiplication; Patterns
2	Division; Decimals—multiplication
3	Decimals—multiplication
4	Multiplication
5	Fractions—addition and subtraction; Graphs, charts, and maps

Week 19

Day	Skills
1	Addition and subtraction; Division
2	Addition and subtraction
3	Time
4	Division
5	Fractions—multiplication and division; Graphs, charts, and maps

Week 20

Day	Skills
1	Addition and subtraction; Multiplication; Linear measurement
2	Multiplication
3	Decimals—addition and subtraction; Decimals—multiplication
4	Division
5	Time; Graphs, charts, and maps; Patterns

Week 21

Day	Skills
1	Fractions—multiplication and division
2	Multiplication
3	Geometry
4	Fractions—addition and subtraction; Weight and capacity
5	Division; Graphs, charts, and maps

Week 22

Day	Skills
1	Perimeter and area
2	Fractions—addition and subtraction
3	Perimeter and area
4	Fractions—multiplication and division
5	Coordinate plane; Graphs, charts, and maps; Patterns

Week 23

Day	Skills
1	Addition and subtraction; Multiplication; Patterns
2	Multiplication; Division; Linear measurement
3	Addition and subtraction; Fractions—addition and subtraction; Fractions—multiplication and division
4	Division
5	Decimals—multiplication; Perimeter and area

Week 24

Day	Skills
1	Fractions—addition and subtraction; Weight and capacity
2	Decimals—addition and subtraction
3	Division; Volume
4	Decimals—division
5	Decimals—place value; Decimals—addition and subtraction

Week 25

Day	Skills
1	Fractions—multiplication and division; Linear measurement
2	Division; Time
3	Division; Time
4	Decimals—multiplication; Decimals—division; Linear measurement; Logical thinking
5	Time; Coordinate plane; Graphs, charts, and maps

Week 26

Day	Skills
1	Addition and subtraction; Multiplication; Division
2	Estimation; Division
3	Addition and subtraction; Multiplication
4	Fractions—multiplication and division
5	Addition and subtraction; Graphs, charts, and maps

Week 27

Day	Skills
1	Division
2	Multiplication; Division; Weight and capacity
3	Decimals—division
4	Fractions—multiplication and division; Weight and capacity
5	Fractions—multiplication and division; Perimeter and area

Week 28

Day	Skills
1	Fractions—multiplication and division; Logical thinking
2	Decimals—place value
3	Patterns
4	Volume
5	Addition and subtraction; Graphs, charts, and maps

Week 29

Day	Skills
1	Multiplication; Decimals—place value; Weight and capacity
2	Fractions—addition and subtraction; Weight and capacity
3	Time
4	Fractions—multiplication and division; Perimeter and area
5	Coordinate plane

Week 30

Day	Skills
1	Division
2	Multiplication; Division; Linear measurement
3	Decimals—addition and subtraction
4	Multiplication; Division
5	Coordinate plane; Graphs, charts, and maps; Logical thinking

Day	Skills
1	Fractions—addition and subtraction
2	Addition and subtraction; Multiplication; Division
3	Multiplication; Division; Fractions—identification and comparison
4	Fractions—multiplication and division
5	Time; Patterns

Week 32

Day	Skills
1	Fractions—addition and subtraction
2	Division; Weight and capacity
3	Addition and subtraction; Multiplication; Division
4	Addition and subtraction; Fractions—addition and subtraction; Patterns
5	Addition and subtraction; Division; Graphs, charts, and maps

Week 33

Day	Skills
1	Addition and subtraction; Multiplication; Fractions—multiplication and division
2	Decimals—multiplication; Perimeter and area
3	Logical thinking
4	Decimals—place value; Decimals—addition and subtraction
5	Addition and subtraction; Multiplication

Week 34

Day	Skills
1	Volume
2	Multiplication; Decimals—place value; Weight and capacity
3	Division; Perimeter and area; Geometry
4	Volume
5	Geometry; Patterns

Week 35

Day	Skills
1	Division; Estimation; Perimeter and area
2	Fractions—identification and comparison
3	Division; Decimals—division; Linear measurement
4	Time
5	Fractions—multiplication and division; Coordinate plane; Graphs, charts, and maps

Week 36

Day	Skills
1	Patterns
2	Fractions—multiplication and division
3	Volume
4	Coordinate plane
5	Logical thinking